THE HAMMARSKJÖLD FORUMS

Case Studies

on

The Role of Law

in the

Settlement of International Disputes

Law and Policy Making for Trade Among "Have" and "Have-Not" Nations

BACKGROUND PAPER AND PROCEEDINGS

of

THE ELEVENTH HAMMARSKJÖLD FORUM

STANLEY D. METZGER
Author of the Working Paper

JOHN CAREY
Editor

Published for

THE ASSOCIATION OF THE BAR OF THE CITY OF NEW YORK

by

OCEANA PUBLICATIONS, INC.
DOBBS FERRY, N. Y.
1968

Library of Congress Catalog Card Number 68-22787
Oceana Book No. 20-11

Table of Contents

THE ELEVENTH HAMMARSKJÖLD FORUM

April 25, 1967

Participants

RAÚL PREBISCH

Secretary-General, United Nations Conference on Trade and Development; formerly Executive Secretary, United Nations Economic Commission for Latin America.

RICHARD N. GARDNER

Henry L. Moses Professor of Law and International Organization, Columbia University; formerly United States Deputy Assistant Secretary of State for International Organization Affairs.

STANLEY D. METZGER

Author of the Working Paper; Professor of Law, Georgetown University Law Center; formerly Assistant Legal Adviser for Economic Affairs, United States Department of State.

Editor's Foreword

The Eleventh Hammarskjöld Forum, held on April 25, 1967, dealt with what U.N. Secretary-General U Thant had called "the most crucial and most challenging long-term struggle of this century," the gap between rich and poor countries. The timeliness of the topic was emphasized by the same official with the approach in early 1968 of the Second U.N. Conference on Trade and Development, when he declared that "...the gap between the rich countries and the poor countries is still getting wider,... It is, in my view, much more basic and much more fundamental to...the future of the peace and security of the world, than the gulf between East and West." In contrast with the East-West ideological gulf, U Thant added, "...in the long run what is much more explosive, is the widening gulf between the North and the South. Unless and until leaders of men and leaders of thought realize this aspect, I am afraid to think of the future. This is one hope I have for the forthcoming second UNCTAD Conference in New Delhi."

Unfortunately the New Delhi Conference caused wide disappointment. The final report of the Conference, which lasted from February 1 to March 29, 1968, acknowledged that, on certain basic issues, "it has been unable, on account of remaining differences of opinion, to reach generally acceptable conclusions." In a closing statement the presiding officer observed that the Conference had not fulfilled the hopes put into it.

Substantive resolutions adopted tended to be vague, such as that citing "unanimous agreement in favour of the early establishment of a mutually acceptable system of generalized non-reciprocal and non-discriminatory preferences which would be beneficial to the developing countries." Another resolution merely recommended that "each economically advanced country should endeavor to provide annually to developing countries financial resource transfers of a minimum net amount of 1 percent of its gross national production at market prices in terms of actual disbursements, having regard to the special position of those countries which are net importers of capital."

1

Lack of progress in closing the gap between the "have" and "have-not" nations is especially disturbing in view of a factor which Dr. Prebisch, three months after the Hammarskjöld Forum, declared to be observable "...in every developing country without exception. I refer to the aspirations of the younger generation, of the dynamic elements of the younger generation, of that group of individuals who have ability, talent and a fighting spirit—in brief, every attribute for rising in the economic and social scale, and who, because of the economy's lack of dynamism and the slow pace of development, are not absorbed into, but remain outside the economic and social process, with a very great sense of frustation. From this standpoint, the difference between a growth rate of 4 or 5 percent and one of 7 or 8 percent is vast. The latter rate is capable of absorbing all these people, while the former will leave them in an increasingly desperate situation. If all the manpower excluded from the modern sector of the economy represents an explosive factor, I would say that the young generation, the dynamic ones, represent the detonator that can spark those explosive elements."

As a means of helping acquaint lawyers with their potential role in the solution of the problems faced at New Delhi and thereafter, the Committee on the Lawyer's Role in the Search for Peace of The Association of The Bar of the City of New York organized one in the series of Hammarskjöld Forums. Participating were the leading personality in the lesser developed countries' drive to improve their economic relations with developed nations, and two prominent American lawyer-economists, each with years of U. S. Government experience and one of whom has since become Chairman of the U. S. Tariff Commission. The material is presented here substantially as it came from the speakers. The Committee believes that this material will add in a valuable way to the literature on law and policy making for trade among "have" and "have-not" nations.

JOHN CAREY, Chairman,
Special Committee on the Lawyer's Role in the Search for Peace, The Association of the Bar of the City of New York

May 1, 1968.

PART ONE

THE WORKING PAPER

Law and Policy Making for Trade Among "Have" and "Have-Not" Nations

Stanley D. Metzger*

There seems to be little question that the intensified striving for economic development of the poorer nations of the world is and has been one of the dominating facts of international life today and for the past ten years. Nor can there be much doubt that this thirst for and thrust toward higher living standards on the part of what Lleras Camargo used to call the "backward" countries, but now referred to as less developed or, even more blandly, "developing" countries, will continue to preoccupy all peoples in the decades ahead as far as one can peer.

It is not surprising that at a time when the obstacles to economic development of the underdeveloped countries appear to be "innumerable and elusive,"[1] there should be all manner of prescriptions advocated for the purpose of helping to achieve sufficient growth so that the peoples of the poorer countries can envision "a promising political and economic alternative to present frustrations, and the hope of moving into a better future."[2]

For economic development involves nothing less than the transformation of a society and its economy. As Prof. Harry G. Johnson, an able and representative member of the modern group of "development economists", has put it somewhat more technically,[3] the development problem is one of converting a "traditional" society predominantly based on "subsistence or near-subsistence agriculture and/or the bulk export of a few primary commodities, in which per capita income grows slowly or may even be declining as a result of population pressure," into a modern society in which "growth of per capita income is internalized in the social and economic system through automatic mechanisms

5

promoting accumulation of capital, improvement of technology, and growth of skill of the labor force."

To create a modern society "capable of self-sustaining economic growth at a reasonable rate" out of an underdeveloped "traditional" one obviously requires deep-seated changes at every turn. Liberation from "colonialism," redistribution of property and income, and economic planning toward material capital accumulation are insufficient prescriptions even in those cases where they are appropriate. Political stability and a "reasonable impartiality of governmental administration to provide an institutional framework for planning innovations," a legal institutional framework to lessen non-economic risks, a social system "permitting mobility of all kinds" and "characterized by the depersonalization of economic and social relationships" in order to provide "maximum opportunities and incentives for individual advancement on the basis of productive economic contribution," are some of the additional requirements.

Indeed, after several centuries of industrialization, preceded by several more of manufacturing and commercial development, it is apparent that this transformation is by no means complete in any of the "developed" countries of the world. About forty million Americans, and very large areas of our country, cannot be characterized as fully participating members of the most affluent society the world has ever known. Accordingly, it should not be surprising that these kinds of changes encounter grave difficulties in less developed countries that have only very recently emerged from tribal levels of organization, as in Africa, or from elaborate and traditional cultures adapted only too well to a nonindustrial way of life, as in Asia, or from colonial cultures derived from eighteenth or nineteenth century European landed-aristocratic cultures already anachronistic when they were implanted, as in Latin America.

More specifically, as the development economists point out, the establishment of a modern economy requires "industrialization"—though it is necessary to state quickly that this means something much wider than the establishment of industries producing manufactures. It means the organization of production in business enterprises, in agriculture as in "industry," characterized by specialization and division of labor, by the application of technology and of mechanical and electrical power to supplement and replace human effort, motivated by the objectives of minimizing costs per unit and maximizing returns to the enterprise. The conscious pursuit of these objectives in a "competitive environment" (and some parts of non-free enterprise systems qualify just as many "free enterprise" systems which are characterized by monopolistic organization of industry do not) leads to capital accumulation, the development and application of new technology, new managerial and marketing methods, and new labor skills, thereby building economic growth automatically into the functioning of the economy. Growth provides expanding opportunities for specialization and division of labor, technical improvements and economies of scale. "Industrialization," therefore, is an economy-wide occurrence, applying to agriculture and the service trades as well as to manufacturing. Its essence is its "rational" approach to the productive process.

Obviously, more than capital investment in industry and in infrastructure is necessary if this kind of industrialization is to happen. A skilled and motivated labor force and professional managerial personnel are required. Both of these demand a particular kind of educational system, in whose creation and development the government must have a very prominent role. Radical changes are needed in the system of land tenure to help transform agriculture into business enterprise; in the distribution of income to create a middle class motivated to accumulate property through saving and to improve its own and its children's economic position by work and education; in systems of taxation and tax collection to increase "productive" savings by instituting progressive tax principles based upon ability to pay in place of the regressive systems now prevalent almost everywhere.

7

This recapitulation of the requirements of modernization—the kinds of fundamental restructuring of the societies of less developed countries necessary to achieve self-sustaining growth—has been made in order to place in proper perspective the various trade and related financial measures which lately have been proffered as conducive to economic development. For the mere recital of these requirements makes clear what all students of the problem have proclaimed—the "transformation must be largely an internal one;"[4] external assistance in no matter what form, while itself ranging in importance from marginal to substantial assistance, plays a subordinate role to internal self-help measures.

No less an advocate of external assistance—and especially assistance in the form of new foreign trade and related economic measures—than Raúl Prebisch has emphasized "the tremendous effort which the developing countries must make to assimilate modern technology cannot be achieved effectively unless these countries, in turn, introduce basic reforms in their economic and social structure."[5] For example, he pointed out, unless "the obsolete system of land tenure...is dealt with forcefully through land reform, technological progress will meet with obstacles that will in many instances prove insurmountable." On a wider front, Mr. Prebisch has emphasized the prime necessity of internal self-help by calling for the overhaul of a social structure which "obstructs social mobility and prevents men of dynamic force from moving up from the bottom to positions of responsibility in the economic life of a country and in its activities generally;" and for the elimination of "outmoded forms of privilege in income distribution... which put no premium on efficiency and are not really conducive to the participation of all members of the nation in the productive process." While he sees education as "a powerful element in social mobility and the rise of capable men to the top," he stresses that "education unaccompanied by a higher growth rate will merely serve to aggravate still

8

further the tension that must arise when the dynamic elements whose wits are sharpened by education and who have been trained for a part in the life of their country are faced with a sluggish rate of development that prevents the full use of their energies in its economic life, thus creating dangerous social and political tensions."

Concluding that "there must be a readiness on the part of developing countries themselves to take a series of sweeping measures, broad and far-reaching, if the world is to achieve an effective development policy," Mr. Prebisch emphasizes, however, that "all these structural reforms— land reforms, reforms conducive to the marshalling of financial and human resources, the campaign against inflation, the deadly poison of inflation which is causing such havoc in a number of developing countries—will be much more difficult to carry out if the economy continues to develop at a sluggish pace." The internal task of social reconstruction will be considerably easier "if income growth rates can be raised not merely to 5 percent, but perhaps to 6, 7, or 8 percent." For high development rates will make it easier "for the developing countries to take the domestic measures required."[6]

To this end of a more rapid growth rate, Mr. Prebisch urges that there be taken "convergent, simultaneous and properly concerted measures" of an international character designed to transfer sufficient resources from the developed to the developing countries in order to assist in improving the growth rate.

We should then examine, however briefly within the limits of reasonable space, the most important of these proposed measures, in order to assess their efficacy in terms of the development problem.

* * * *

Substantial efforts have been made since the close of World War II to transfer resources directly from the richer

9

to the poorer countries in order to foster economic development. There have been multilateral lending agencies such as the International Bank for Reconstruction and Development, the Inter-American Development Bank, the International Development Association, the new Asian Development Bank, and the United Nations' Special Fund; bilateral American programs such as the lending and granting activities of the Export-Import Bank and the various AID programs; bilateral foreign programs: the French and British loan and grant programs to their respective former colonial territories (and the few which remain under formal political tutelage), the Japanese loan and grant programs in the form of reparations and successor programs, the German loan program (largely in the form of short to medium term export credits); and loose co-ordinating or aid-policy discussion centers such as the Colombo Plan and the Development Assistance Committee of the Organization for Economic Cooperation and Development.[7]

Nonetheless, it is clear that the amount of resources transferred has been insufficient to move the overwhelming number of less developed countries to a position of "self-sustaining growth."[8] This has led to a renewed double-pronged effort by the less developed countries, acting in greater unison than hitherto, aimed at securing more direct foreign assistance in the form of loans and grants, and as a newer element, indirect foreign aid in the form of various trade measures.

The first branch of this effort—increased direct foreign aid—was publicized in 1960 as the "United Nations Development Decade." It had as its goal that less developed countries attain by 1970 a minimum annual growth rate in aggregate national income of 5 percent, and, as its principal external assistance component, a foreign aid contribution of 1% of the gross national product of each of the developed countries.[9] Actually, this goal was modest enough, measured by the task of development.[10] One example suffices: at the outset of the Development Decade, Pakistan, in 1960,

10

adopted a five-year plan estimated to cost $4 billion, of which she hoped to raise 60 percent domestically and 40 percent, amounting to $1,680 million, from foreign sources. If successful, Pakistan asserted, the plan might enable her to raise per capita income from $50 to $55 a year by the end of 1965.[11]

But the portents for increased foreign aid were not especially good in the earliest part of our present decade, and steadily became worse. The 1% goal has been missed by a wide margin.[12] And we are now witnessing the rather unedifying spectacle of our country responding slowly and conditionally to the supplications of its own appointee, the able President of the IBRD, who is seeking additional funds for IDA. The reasons for the current disheartening prospects for increased direct aid are varied: disenchantment with the results of past efforts; balance of payments problems in the United States, which has been and remains the principal supplier of foreign aid; American preoccupation with the Vietnam War, which is related of course to balance of payments considerations; and lessened tension with the Soviet Union, rendering less urgent the need to expand expenditures for palpably political short-term ends. This, of course, is no sort of catalog.

In addition, the less developed countries, most of whom had recently emerged from various forms of political tutelage into political independence, faced with a sluggish increase of exports because of fallen prices of many basic commodities,[13] were anxious to change the form of foreign aid from the bilateral client-state relationship, with its inevitable political and economic strings.[14] Multi-lateral direct loans and grants from richer to poorer nations were of course more consonant with political independence than bilateral aid, because there were fewer political and economic conditions,[15] and were therefore to be preferred. But, as noted, it was becoming increasingly more difficult to get multilateral aid in desired quantities, and repayments of aid extended in the past, both multilateral and

11

bilateral, were becoming a very substantial and onerous offset.[16] If, so went the thought, aid could be framed in more indirect forms, perhaps it might be somewhat more palatable in domestic political terms for developed countries to extend it; after all, direct income payments somehow have seemed, to the uniniated in developed countries, to be more of a subsidy than high, rigid price supports, non-recourse loans, and high prices for domestic agricultural products. At the same time, since aid in such indirect forms might not sound like loans or grants, it might become more difficult for the developed countries to exact political or even economic "terms" when extending it.

This meant that the second prong of the attack upon economic development was in the form of international measures relating to trade whose aim was the transfer of resources from the richer to the poorer nations in an amount greater than is consequent upon the "ordinary" workings of the markets in goods.

The movement in this direction, now well underway, may be said to have begun officially in 1962, when the Economic and Social Council of the United Nations called for a United Nations Conference on Trade and Development.[17] While it recognized "the importance of increasing the net inflow of long term capital to developing countries and improving its terms and conditions," the thrust of the resolution was "the vital importance of the rapid growth of exports and export earnings of developing countries, of primary products and manufacturers, for promoting their economic development." Calling attention to the "drop in prices of primary commodities" in recent years, and the worsening in the terms of trade of developing countries with developed countries (relatively lower prices received for imports than are paid for manufactured imports),[18] ECOSOC emphasized that "measures to impart stability in international commodity markets at remunerative levels" are "vital" to less developed countries. This presaged an intensified drive for commodity agreements.

12

In addition, the ECOSOC resolution called attention to "the importance of all countries and all regional and subregional economic groupings pursuing trade policies designed to facilitate the necessary expansion of trade of developing countries and encouraging the indispensable growth of their economies." This presaged, somewhat more obscurely, the effort to secure tariff preferences from developed countries for the manufacturers of the less developed countries, and a more intensified effort to perfect regional preference schemes, whether full scale customs unions and free-trade areas, or partial commodity or product preference schemes.

When the General Assembly in 1962 endorsed the ECOSOC Resolution, it elaborated these points and expanded them in several particulars: it called for "international compensatory financing" for shortfalls in expectations of exchange earnings from the sale of primary commodities; and for the increase in consumption of "semimanufactured and manufactured goods imported from developing countries," which rather obliquely called for a diminution in protectionism in developed countries of the manufactured products most important to less developed countries, such as textiles, leather, wood products, toys, and sporting goods.[19]

While a later resolution in 1963, the report of the Secretary General of the Conference, Mr. Prebisch, in March 1964, and the Final Act of the Conference in June 1964, elaborated upon these points, and added a few others, such as less developed countries' participation in shipping and other "invisible" items important to foreign trade, the current major preoccupations of UNCTAD, which was made a permanent organ of the U.N. General Assembly by its resolution of December 30, 1964,[20] were very clearly foreshadowed by the ECOSOC 1962 resolution recommending the calling of the Conference. We will now turn to these specific proposed trade measures.

I. COMMODITY AGREEMENTS

"Exports of primary products are at the present time the overwhelmingly important source of earnings of foreign exchange and receipts of external resources by the less developed countries, accounting for some 85-90 percent of their total export earnings.[21] It is clear then that despite the great amount of attention which has been paid recently to tariff preferences for manufactured goods, and to regional mechanisms for increased trade among less developed countries, (which look largely to increased intra-regional trade in manufactures), the major contribution to (or subtraction from) the economic development of developing countries attributable to foreign trade for a long time to come will depend upon the earnings from the sale to developed countries of primary commodities, agricultural and mineral, produced by less developed countries.

When the basic conceptions of the post-war trading world were being framed in Havana in the Charter of the International Trade Organization[22] and in Geneva in the General Agreement on Tariffs and Trade,[23] the core idea was freeing international trade from artificial barriers to its increase, whether of a governmental or private nature. Reduction of such barriers to the trade of goods would lead to production and distribution on the basis of comparative advantage in their production, to lower prices, to higher effective demand and living standards, and in consequence, to higher levels of trade and of economic growth.

Cartels, fixing prices and manipulating production and distribution for that purpose, constituted, at least so far as industrial products were concerned, just such an artificial barrier which was inconsistent with trade on the basis of comparative advantage, and the ITO Charter would have legislated against them whenever they had adverse effects upon international trade.[24] For experience with them had demonstrated that consumers within a country, and, internationally, countries themselves, paid more for goods so

14

price-fixed than the prices they otherwise would have commanded, and that the curtailment of production involved in order to keep the price "stable" (and high enough to keep the marginal producer in the black at all times) almost always erred on the restrictive side. In the bargain, the benefits to the industry were distributed indifferently if at all; and, so far as the countries were concerned, if they received any benefits in the form of investment of the fruits of monopoly pricing (rather than Swiss bank accounts and Riviera real estate) these were haphazard in character.[25]

But what about the primary commodities? Would the difficulties of the "free market" outweigh its virtues, unlike what then-dominant opinion believed regarding industrial products? Would the very wide price fluctuations of many of the primary commodities have such social repercussions in one or two crop countries as to call for greater tolerance of "monopolistic combination of the cartel type?"[26] The majority at Havana clearly thought so, even though all recognized that the pre-war private cartels which had operated in the primary commodity field had been far from happy ventures from the viewpoint of the consumer and, indeed, of the producer countries.[27] The International Tin Committee, for example, composed exclusively of tin producing countries (whose spokesmen were the tin producing companies, which were interlocking in a classic sense) consistently had restricted tin production in the interest of higher prices to such an extent, at times to 33-1/3 and 35% of "standard" production in each country,[28] that there were substantial physical shortages when World War II broke out.

J. P. F. Rowe, in his excellent book, "Primary Commodities in International Trade" (Cambridge, 1965), found that in 1945 there was "broad agreement that commodity policy should have three main aims"—an expanding world economy with an increasing production and consumption of material wealth, a "reasonable stability of prices about the current long-period trend," and "reasonably appro-

15

priate and stable incomes to primary producers."[29] The Havana Charter, however, framed the consensus somewhat more narrowly. While recognizing that there might be a "tendency towards persistent disequilibrium between production and consumption," and an "accumulation of burdensome stocks and pronounced fluctuations in prices" which could adversely affect producers and consumers, "jeopardizing the general policy of economic expansion," the Charter nonetheless required that there be a "burdensome surplus," in being or expected to develop, or "widespread unemployment or under-employment," in being or expected, before a commodity control agreement could be countenanced.[30] Even then, it must be an agreement among governments, not private parties; it must offer membership to consuming as well as producing countries, and provide each, as a group, equal weight in decision-making under the agreement; and, finally, the duration of any price-controlling agreement must be limited to five years so that a new reading as to the necessity for any continuation be taken at relatively short intervals.[31]

The general theoretical point of view, then, as reflected in the ITO Charter, was that commodity control was acceptable only as a "necessary evil" to prevent hardship to small producers and wage-earners when normal market forces could not be relied upon to do so.

But even at that time this cannot be said to have been the real point of view of the producing interests which, through governments, have brought about the negotiation of commodity agreements in a limited number of commodities in the past twenty years. The post-war agreements in tin, wheat, sugar, and coffee had a long pre-war history going back to schemes in the 1920s and 1930s. Most of their proponents believed (and privately made no secret about their views) that the trade in their commodities required control in the longest run foreseeable; they were also by no means satisfied to "preserve a reasonable stability of prices about the current long-period trend."[32]

16

At all events, the conflicts in economic interest between producing and consuming countries, the fear that price stabilization at levels somewhat higher than the trend would encourage growth in production of substitutes (i.e. synthetic rubber), the serious technical problems involved in creating workable commodity agreements (i.e., the difficulties in predicting long-term price trends, and in securing agreement upon the relationship of a buffer stock to market operations)—these knotty problems meant both that a variety of techniques of control needed to be improvised and that the number of "successful" negotiations would be small.

The commodity control devices have been quite varied: a "collective contract" (wheat) by which exporters agreed to sell at the ceiling and consuming countries to buy at the floor of a wide price swing in order to contain prices within that range; a straight export quota control device, policed by consuming countries in the form of import restrictions (coffee), designed to hold the price at the 1962 level (which one commentator has charged is "a level which was roughly double the price at which Brazil, by far the largest producer, could profitably supply more than her export quota under the agreement");[33] an export quota scheme buttressed by a small buffer stock (tin).

The fate of the four commodity agreements which were negotiated, so far as "stability" is concerned, has not been very happy. As Rowe has aptly summarized it, the sugar scheme has been suspended; the tin agreement has lost control more than once and is presently, and for some time has been, without effect on the market; the coffee agreement has had indifferent success in achieving price stability. The record in wheat is better, but because the U.S. and Canada have pegged the price through mutual agreement and not as a consequence of the agreement's operations.[34] There is little doubt, though, that coffee prices have been maintained at higher levels than would have prevailed in the absence of agreement.

17

The new element in commodity agreements policy introduced by the less developed countries prior to UNCTAD, and pointedly stressed there and elsewhere since 1964, is a conscious change in purpose from that of price "stabilization" to one of price augmentation in order to secure higher levels of export earnings for developing countries as a whole than they would receive were prices to be stabilized around the long-term trend.[35]

Commodity control schemes are now viewed as instruments for stabilizing prices at the highest possible level—as a form of aid from the richer consuming countries to the poorer primary producing countries.[36] In short, they are to be the international counterpart of familiar domestic agricultural interventions such as high, rigid price supports financed through artificially high consumer prices, which means that those least able to pay bear the greatest burden of supporting welfare measures.

This change in the conception of commodity agreements is important in several different respects.

In the first place, it clearly identifies them as aid mechanisms either supplementary to or in substitution of direct financial assistance in the form of loans or grants, immediately raising the question whether they are an efficient means of aid-giving or "disastrous to the world's economy and to the growth of the world's wealth at the maximum rate."[37] To those economists who believe that "it is a fundamental economic principle that prices should be related to cost of production," and that if they are not, "resources are being wasted somewhere," a policy of "trade at artificially high prices" is "bound to lead to the waste and misuse of the world's limited resources and cannot maximize the world's wealth." Some become eloquent with rage:

"If the supply of primary products is restricted below what the world should have, as shown by the measuring rod of cost, the whole economic system of the world becomes twisted and warped, and cannot function with maximum efficiency. Admittedly some countries may succeed for a time in snatch-

18

ing a temporary advantage, but that can only be at the expense of others. The use and adaptation of commodity control schemes deliberately to secure artificially high prices is a throwback to the worst examples of controls in the inter-war period, such as the British rubber restriction scheme and Copper Exporters, Inc.,[38] it is the negation of the ideas and doctrines on which the Havana Charter—United Nations conception of the proper uses of commodity control schemes was built; it amounts to the prostitution of control schemes as instruments for the proper stabilization of prices."[39]

On the other hand, there are other economists who, while not particularly liking these agreements, support them because they appear to despair of seeing the world deal in economically sensible terms with its economic problems, and are therefore prepared to see economically-distorting devices employed in order to get more aid to developing countries.[40]

Secondly, this new conception of the role of commodity agreements narrows even more severely the possible number of commodities which might be candidates for eventual agreements of the true "stabilizing" type. A recent UNCTAD study[41] distinguished three categories of primary commodities by their market characteristics. The first group comprise commodities produced wholly or mainly in developing countries and not subject to competition from substitutes, such as coffee. The second consists of commodities produced wholly or mainly in developing countries but subject to competition from substitutes, especially synthetics (e.g. natural rubber). The third relates to commodities produced in substantial quantities by both developed and developing countries (sugar).

As Prof. Isaiah Frank has pointed out,[42] agreements aimed at raising prices "can be effective in increasing producers' incomes mainly with respect to commodities in the first group, for which somewhat higher prices will not significantly reduce demand." Regarding the second group, however, "higher prices for the natural product would be self-defeating, since the result would be to encourage further substitution." What is required here are not high-price commodity control schemes but "cost reductions to improve the competitive position of the natural product, and diversification over the longer term into production with more favorable market prospects." Concerning the third group, commodities produced in both developing and developed countries, the "main problems arise from import barriers in the advanced countries." Here, he adds, the "principal aim of policy should be to increase the access of low-income countries to the high-income markets," through the elimination or drastic curtailment of protectionist import quotas designed to insulate domestic high-cost producers from competition.

This means that the "scope for commodity price-fixing arrangements as a means of raising the export earnings of developing countries is quite limited." Five major commodities only fit into the first group: coffee, tea, cocoa, bananas and tin. In 1964, exports of these commodities amounted to about 12 percent of the total exports of developing countries, but if coffee and tin are excluded, because commodity agreements already exist for them, the remaining products account for only about 4 percent of exports. If one then excludes tea, which was the subject of a commodity agreement among producing countries only from 1950-1955, in fact was not an important factor in the market, and so far has not moved to stage center; and bananas, whose marketing problems are made no easier these days of increasing awareness of obesity—we are left with cocoa.

Indeed, cocoa is the commodity which has been preoccupying UNCTAD these past several years since the abortive conference of October 1963. The difficulty then was the floor price, which producing countries desired to have established at a level which *The Economist* termed "unrealistically high," precisely because of their need for aid to developing countries.[43] At present, in the light of succeeding but as yet unsuccessful further conferences and consultations, the floor price question is still unsolved, as is the question of the financing and the operation of a proposed buffer stock. Consuming countries are being asked to contribute substantially to the financing of a buffer stock, unlike the situation in the tin agreement, where the producing countries bore the entire burden.[44]

In all events, it seems clear that regardless of the outcome of the cocoa talks, the prospect of further commodity agreements of the "price-raising" type, even more than of the "stabilizing" kind, appears to be dim.

In terms of maximizing earnings from trade, it might well be far more productive for the developing countries to change their apparent current direction and press much harder than they have done in the recent past for the elimination or drastic curtailment of the protective devices still maintained by developed countries over cotton, sugar and the other commodities in the production of which developing countries enjoy a comparative advantage. In these terms, the developing countries have an excellent case on economic principle, and they have as allies within the developed countries all those who have fought for years to create and maintain a liberal trade policy bottomed upon non-discrimination and the steady reduction of all artificial barriers to an increase in international trade on the basis of comparative advantage in production and distribution of goods.

For it is very doubtful that the less developed countries can press successfully for both types of measures. It would be too easy for the protectionist forces in the developed countries to defeat the effort to reduce protection in those developed countries if at the same time as the developing countries were asking for access on liberal trade lines in these important exchange-earning areas, they were working the other side of the street—seeking monopoly pricing— for the non-substitutable primary commodities which they produce, through the "new" commodity agreement route. An effort to secure both objectives could too easily lead to that most unhappy of results—developing countries losing where they should win (through reducing protectionism in

21

richer countries), and, if they were lucky, scoring the most Pyrrhic of victories where their case was quite poor. In addition, their case for more direct financial assistance—which could not be better and should be pushed with maximum strength—would suffer because part of the effort needed to secure such increased assistance would have been expended in attempting to secure commodity agreements.

II. COMPENSATORY FINANCING

The second aspect of the international trade approach to measures for improving the position of the primary commodity-exporting, less developed countries, has come to be known as "compensatory financing." As has been noted, the commodity agreement approach has been seen by many to have been of limited utility during the past twenty years. In the late 1950's, at a time when export earnings accruing primarily from international commodity sales had become sluggish, not rising in quantity or totals as fast as was necessary to maintain imports needed for economic development, the idea became current that there should be made available to developing countries financial resources to compensate for fluctuations in foreign exchange receipts from the export of primary commodities. The thought was that economic development required planning, planning required a relatively constant expectation of exchange earnings from "normal" commodity exports, and hence that recourse to an international facility for such compensatory finance, tied to a shortfall in anticipated earnings, was closely related to, and only a somewhat indirect form of, straight financial foreign aid.

Beginning in 1960, and continuing to the present, the idea and the practice of compensatory financing have gained currency, through prodding by UNCTAD and otherwise, and further developments are anticipated. A principal reason for the progress in this area is that compensatory financing, like the more traditional forms of direct loans and grants, does not interfere with the normal market forces connected with the sale and distribution of goods, and hence does not carry with it side effects which can be harmful.

To date this progress has been in the form of responses in 1963[45] and 1966[46] by the International Monetary Fund to requests for favorable action by the U.N. Commission on International Commodity Trade in 1960, and by many countries at the UNCTAD meeting in 1964 and thereafter. These Fund responses also took account of studies by the U.N. Committee of Experts in 1961,[47] and by the Organization of American States Group of Experts in 1962.[48]

It should be noted that as early as 1960 the Fund had stated as a matter of policy that member countries "that are taking appropriate steps to preserve internal financial stability and to maintain their balance of payments in equilibrium, taking good years with bad, ... can anticipate with confidence that financing will be available from the Fund which, in conjunction with a reasonable use of their own reserves, should be sufficient to enable them to overcome temporary payments difficulties arising from export fluctuations."[49] In 1963, noting that "trends in prices of basic commodities in the past few years have adversely affected the export earnings of many fund members, which has increased the strain on their reserves," the Fund liberalized its system of loans—"drawings"—to compensate for such export earnings shortfalls. A member might draw up to 25 percent of its quota to compensate for export shortfalls of a "short-term character" which was "largely attributable to circumstances beyond" its control, the fact of a "shortfall" being determined by a calculation of the "medium term trend" in prices of the commodity over a five-year moving average.[50] The Fund also indicated it would approve quota increases for developing countries with small quotas.

Some twenty countries availed themselves of this latter privilege, and three (Brazil and the United Arab Republic in 1963, and Sudan in 1965) of the new drawing rights. While this is not a particularly intensive use of the new facilities, perhaps it is explicable by the "improvement in commodity markets after the new facility had been established, and . . . the initial reluctance of countries to prejudice their access to ordinary fund drawings."[51]

In 1966 the Fund expanded the compensatory financing facility.[52] Instead of drawings up to 25 percent, drawings up to 50 percent of a member's quota to offset export shortfalls may be made, but in the absence of "disasters or major emergencies"[53] not more than 25 percent in any one year. As Prof. Frank has observed, these drawings are additional to a country's normal borrowing rights in the Fund, are available on "virtually automatic terms," and no longer affect the conditions under which members have access to ordinary drawings; they are, however, repayable in three to five years, like ordinary drawings.[54]

The Fund's efforts do not exhaust the possibilities of compensatory financing. Following an invitation by UNCTAD consequent upon a United Kingdom-Swedish proposal, the IBRD staff at the end of 1965 submitted a specific scheme to the United Nations dealing with the problems arising from "unexpected adverse movements" in the export proceeds of developing countries which are of a "nature or duration which cannot be dealt with by short-term balance of payments support," but require longer-term assistance to help in avoiding disruption of development programs.

This IBRD "Supplementary Financing" scheme, which is quite literally envisioned as "supplementary to and not a substitute for already existing forms of aid," is estimated by the World Bank to require between $300 and $400 million per year to operate over an experimental period of five years. To be eligible to receive support, a country would have to enter into a prior agreement with the administering agency on sound development programs and policies "prior to the time of need." If the country lived up to its policy commitments and had no other readily available source of finance, long-term loans would be made to make

24

up for a deficiency of exports as compared to the agreed reasonable expectations.

The Bank's study, a major and imaginative initiative in foreign aid, is based upon a number of articulated premises.[55] Uncertainty is inevitable in economic development programming—the scheme aims at removing one source of uncertainty, the effects of "marked unforeseen adverse movements" in export receipts. The Bank's study asserts that the "familiar problems of the instability and sluggish growth" of export receipts of developing countries "can in the long run only be solved through sustained development and diversification of the production and exports of primary product exporting countries." But by "helping to assure a continuous growth process," the scheme can contribute to this basic solution. While developing countries which encounter a "foreseeable" deterioration in export receipts because of reasons beyond their control will need long-term foreign capital to bridge the foreign exchange gap until the process of development places their economies on a self-sustaining basis, this must be dealt with under existing aid mechanisms; the scheme is limited to uncertainty in export receipts owing to "marked unforeseen adverse movements" in export receipts.

UNCTAD has convened an Intergovernmental Group on Supplementary Financing to consider the World Bank's scheme. It has had two inconclusive sessions, the last having been held in Geneva from Feb. 6-17, 1967.

Thus far all of the major elements of the scheme appear to be undergoing intensive and critical examination by the UNCTAD Group: whether assistance should be more or less automatic or based to a greater extent on the discretion of the agency; whether the crucial element—an agreed "policy package" with the agency—involves "undue interference" in the affairs of the developing country concerned the method for calculating export projections and for revising them; the costs of the scheme—whether $300-$4 million a year is realistic; and whether it is possible to li commitments of donor countries.[56] These and a number of other issues indicate that it would be unwise to expect the fruition of a Supplementary Financing scheme any time soon.

The IMF compensatory financing facilities of 1963 and 1966 and the IBRD's proposed Supplementary Financing scheme are important developments, however, even beyond the financial assistance that they can render to developing countries dependent, as almost all are and will continue overwhelmingly to be, upon exports of primary commodities. For they bespeak what seems to be a healthy, growing "realization that individual stabilization arrangements [commodity agreements] are at best suitable for only a handful of commodities, and that, in addition, such schemes are likely to have only limited success in achieving their objectives."[57] And they indicate that, in the primary commodity area at least, the developing countries are coming to the view that real transfers of resources from richer to poorer countries which benefit a large number of the poorer countries—and the poorest among them—might better be secured through direct mechanisms which interfere as little as possible with a market whose long-run sensitivity to the permutations of the world's economy has yet to be rivalled by efforts to deal piecemeal and episodically with some of its special aspects.

III. PREFERENCES

Probably no proposal advanced by spokesmen for developing countries at the 1964 UNCTAD Conference, and continuously urged since then, has been subjected to as much debate, some of it acrimonious, as preferences in the markets of developed countries for the manufacturers and semi-manufacturers of the less developed countries.[58]

The reason is not hard to find. The central conception of the postwar trading world, envisaged during and immediately following World War II and carried through in the General Agreement on Tariffs and Trade in 1947, was

26

non-discrimination in trade—unconditional most-favored-nation treatment. In this respect, as is almost always the case, general international agreement was the capstone of an arch long under construction through national laws. Beginning in 1923, the United States embarked upon "unconditional" most-favored-nation clauses in its commercial treaties,[59] and in the 1934 Trade Agreements Act made non-discrimination mandatory as a matter of domestic statute, which it has continued to be down to the present time.[60] European countries had adopted the unconditional form of most-favored-nation clause much earlier; by the 20th century all the important countries were adherents.

While complete customs unions and free trade areas, very few of which had been consummated, were viewed as exceptions to the rule, and preferences for colonial territories' goods (almost all primary commodities) in metropole markets were tolerated though decried, only the former, safeguarded by new conditions, continued to be encouraged by GATT. The former colonial preference arrangements were frozen by GATT—no increase in the margins could be made—and no further preferences were permitted. This was not because there was a judgment that they were a good thing—quite the contrary. But an international agreement cannot be overly ambitious; it must often accept what exists, however grudgingly, and legislate against repetition in the future, much as a price control law must often eschew a "rollback." Any idea that since GATT's inhospitality to preference schemes did not lead it to legislate against the 1947 remnants of the colonial arrangements, it was somehow smiling benignly upon new preferences between developed and developing countries, as has been indicated by some who are attempting to create a favorable climate of opinion for preferences, is plainly wrong.

The basic GATT approach to trade—non-discrimination, elimination of quotas on imports, and continuous reduction of tariffs through mutual concessional bargaining—

has never been insensitive to the development needs of less developed countries, even though GATT's role is predominantly oriented to sensible relationships in trade amongst developed countries.[61] It simply stands for the proposition that the best way to accomplish the most effective allocation of the world's resources, internationally, is through free trade, supplemented by straight aid to developing countries. No less a friend of almost any measure to assist less developed countries than Harry G. Johnson has argued that the "best solution to the problem of providing additional external resources for the acceleration of development would be free trade, plus the provision of aid on a scale determined either by the net resources required to support rates of growth in the less developed countries endorsed by the developed countries, or by the amounts of resources agreed on by the developed countries to be necessary to fulfill their commitments to the less developed countries."[62] Protectionism, he asserts, is not in the interest of developed countries because "in all its manifold varieties," it "wastes their resources and impedes their own growth." So far as less developed countries are concerned, preferences are an "inefficient means" of securing "more net aid from the developed countries, or improved access to developed-country markets."[63]

Market access for manufactured products of developing countries—now significant for only a small number (Hong Kong, India, Mexico, Taiwan, Pakistan, the Philippines)—could be secured more efficiently through quota increases or tariff reductions. Even the apparent exception to his conclusion—Mr. Prebisch's extension of the "infant-industry"[64] argument into a case for preferences in industrial products—Johnson believes could be accommodated by applying an economically efficient policy for genuine infant industries—one which would subsidize infant-industry production "as a social investment in a socially profitable learning process." This subsidy should be "financed through the development program and hence enter into the reckoning of net foreign aid requirements."

28

Partly because protectionism in developed countries is difficult to get rid of, partly because more aid is hard to come by, less developed countries have looked for partial solutions in the field of expansion of manufactured exports. This is in consequence of their concern that the long-term prospects for most of the basic commodities in which they specialize are not encouraging. They believe that they must increasingly become exporters of manufactured products, both because it would lead to more rapid export expansion and because of its "linkage" effect in inducing investment in related sectors of the economy. While recently manufactured exports from developing countries have increased markedly (14 percent annually, 1960-1964), the absolute volume is quite low and confined to the small number of countries indicated hitherto.

The main difficulties in expanding exports of manufactures have been described as "restrictions imposed by the advanced countries, and questionable policies in the developing countries themselves."[65] In the former category are higher tariffs on processed goods than tariff averages tend to describe, and more "effective" tariffs the greater degree of processing of raw materials;[66] and quota controls on certain very important manufactures in which some developing countries enjoy a comparative advantage in production, notably textiles. In the latter category are excessive import substitution schemes in less developed countries, which tend to increase costs of production of all goods, including exportable manufactures.

While the developing countries have tended lately, through stressing the importance of "effective" tariffs, to dramatize the extent to which tariffs in developed countries may still be high enough to inhibit their manufactured exports, they have been relatively quiescent in submitting, along with some developed countries such as Japan, to what Prof. Frank has characterized as "the most restrictive set of barriers to processed exports confronting the low-income countries"—the 5-year Long-Term Cotton Textile Arrange-

29

ment of 1962, which very recently has been extended for another 3 years. This agreement, which restrains textile exports from less developed countries in the interest of avoiding "market disruption" in developed countries, has become "the vehicle through which highly restrictive quotas have been imposed—in Europe as well as in the United States—with little regard to the criteria for determining the existence of market disruption."[67] In contrast, the interest of developing countries in "preferential, rather than simply equal, access" for their processed and manufactured goods to the markets of advanced countries has been expressed with growing tenacity.

The arguments for and against preferences, putting aside for the moment the precise nature of the preference, have been summarized by John Pincus, who in general can be counted a friend of preferences.[68]

The case for preferences he puts as follows:

(1) the future gains accruing to the less developed countries from further trade liberalization are uncertain, both in respect of the Kennedy Round because of exceptions,[69] and thereafter;

(2) even if those gains were forthcoming and large, infant-industry and "equity" grounds conspire to warrant further concessions;

(3) the income transfer involved in making price concessions to the less developed countries is small but is more acceptable politically to donor and recipient than the equivalent foreign aid subsidy;

(4) many less developed countries have gone as far as—and often farther than—they should in import substitution, so that any device to encourage export promotion is desirable;

(5) the less developed countries want preferences and the developed countries' costs from granting them "would be negligible, whether or not the alleged gains materialize."

It is noteworthy that the great emphasis of the arguments has been placed on the circumstance that developing countries want preferences, and very little on their economic importance.

The arguments against preferences Pincus delineates as follows:

(1) they tend to promote and perpetuate economic inefficiency—even those arguments of the infant-industry and scale-economy type which are valid are grounds for subsidy rather than preference;

(2) rather than improving relations between poorer and richer nations, preferential systems would exacerbate them for a variety of reasons—they "invariably discriminate" in effect against some less developed countries, they would create an automatic obstacle toward further efforts to liberalize world trade (because reduction of tariffs also reduces the preference margin), and they would, if successful, create a type of economic dependence on concessions from developed countries that is "inconsistent with" the developing countries' "struggle for independence;"

(3) preferential systems are strikingly complicated to administer in any event;

(4) preferences are likely to bring with them the reverse of the effects intended, because the introduction of preferences gives domestic producers in developed countries a chance to legislate restrictive safeguards that would be more difficult under a non-discriminatory tariff policy; these might well leave the developing countries with less access than they had before;

(5) the gains from preferential systems would be small, because tariffs, even effective tariffs, are generally low now in light of the less developed countries' cost disadvantage, and may be lower after the Kennedy Round is completed;

(6) preferences are an inferior way to give aid and lead to an inequitable distribution of aid costs.

31

A few further words may be in order regarding (2) immediately above, relating to the type of preferences envisaged, and the consequences. The UNCTAD idea has been a "non-discriminatory" system of discrimination in favor of all less developed countries, i.e., the duty on Widget A is generally 15% ad valorem in England, but those from less developed countries (as defined) should pay zero duty.[70] The chance of securing this kind of general and uniform preference is very small. The African former colonies of the countries forming the European Economic Community, for example, now enjoy a preference for their manufactures (and their raw materials) in the EEC market by virtue of their "association" with the EEC. While thus far this preference has meant extremely little in trade terms,[71] any idea that these countries are likely to give up this special preference for a general one applicable to all developed countries, very likely to do them even less good, must be considered a non-starter. In fact, they have already so indicated. Rather nebulous talk about "compensating" them somehow for this switch is likely to continue to fall upon deaf ears.

Moreover, not only those less developed countries who stand to gain very little from a generalized preference scheme (meaning the great majority[72]) are likely to be recalcitrant. EEC countries put forward at UNCTAD in 1964 the Belgian "Brasseur Plan," supported by France.[73] Under this plan, the terms of preference (the preferential margin, the duration of preference, and the quantity of imports to which the preference applies) would be negotiated for each commodity. As Harry G. Johnson put it, perhaps hyperbolically, the "administrative and diplomatic cumbersomeness" of this plan, and "its inherent risks of political and economic dependence" of particular less developed on particular developed countries "appalled" the vast majority of representatives present.[74] Johnson indicates the complications conceivably ensuing from any such scheme:[75] "On the basis of twenty developed nations and seventy less devel-

32

oped nations, one thousand products would require nearly one and a half million bilateral negotiations. Many of these negotiations, of course, would not be worthwhile to the individual less developed countries; on the other hand, the number of tariff items on which negotiations might be worthwhile for one or more pairs of countries is obviously many times one thousand."

Apart from these complications, what about the results of such a selective approach to preferences by the EEC, which has been stated to be favorable to preferences "in principle?"

Results cannot be foretold, of course, in advance of negotiations, but since the selective approach is quite obviously designed to take into account the interests of domestic producers and former overseas territories, to say nothing of important third countries which might become disenchanted with preferential competition and decide to cut back on EEC imports, is it too far-fetched to suggest, as one skeptic did recently, that in any negotiations the less developed countries might well succeed in securing preferences for left-handed catchers' mitts and solid-gold Cadillacs?

Lastly, were the less developed countries to succeed in securing some tariff preferences which would benefit a relatively small number of countries, in a relatively small range of products, they would in all likelihood be paying an economic and a political price which they may not have fully appreciated. Since developed countries would consider that they were providing "what is essentially additional foreign aid under the guise of expansion of trade opportunities,"[76] it would be natural for them to take this into account as an offset to straight foreign aid, and, in addition, to exact whatever political and economic conditions appear to them to be suitable from time to time, ranging from tied loans to non-trading with Cuba, from special conditions on nationalization to 50-50 shipping, as well as others too numerous to mention which might seem to be dictated by the exigencies of the moment. A trading world further rent asunder on this basis would tend to resemble nothing so much as the immediate pre-war trading world which one had thought it had been resolved to avoid at almost any cost.

IV. REGIONAL ARRANGEMENTS

Regional arrangements such as the Latin American Free Trade Area, and the Central American Common Market, while not immediately and primarily addressed to trade between richer and poorer nations, nonetheless affect trade between the developed and the less developed countries and accordingly call for some comment.

They are an effort at what might be termed "collective import substitution" through the creation of a wider customs territory and hence a wider internal market. The hope is that this wider market will induce greater investment to take advantage of economies of scale, and divert present outside sources of supplies, mainly of machinery and other developmental manufacturers, to new or newly-expanded internal sources, as well as to cause a shift from high to lower cost sources within the area. Because existing domestic markets in such areas are believed to offer only to entrepreneurs with a virtual monopoly the opportunities to reach the size needed to adopt modern production techniques, a wider market could enhance productivity and growth by enlarging opportunities for scale economies. This in turn could create a deeper market, if monopoly pricing and the siphoning-off of higher profits to non-productive investments or safehavens could be avoided.

However, as has been pointed out by Patterson,[77] each developing country appears to be looking for increased production of manufactured goods—to be seeking "industrialization" in the narrower sense of the term—more than it is seeking productivity increases. None enjoys an atmosphere in which competition is favored, and few have been able to ensure that earnings are invested at home in productive enterprise. In addition, if each member of a regional

34

arrangement is to increase its exports more than its imports there must be trade diversion from outside sources. To the extent that this might result in higher real economic costs throughout the region, the regional arrangement could eventuate as considerably less than a major contribution to economic well-being.

Nonetheless, just as the skepticism toward large claims for customs unions and free trade areas for relatively developed countries, expressed by economists such as Viner, Robbins, and Hawtrey, has not carried the day because of political reasons in the case of EEC and EFTA,[78] so the even greater skepticism concerning the relative importance to development of regionalism among less developed countries has not caused outside countries to discourage its burgeoning. In fact it has become easier for outside developed countries to encourage regionalism for developing countries than to remain enthusiastic about developed country regional arrangements, whose policies have begun to cause actual economic problems.[78a] There are not only the usual political reasons for not standing in the way of efforts by the less developed countries to trade more with each other, but there are practically no important economic reasons for an adverse position for a long time to come. Indeed, a cynic could say that it is a very "soft option"[79] for developed countries to encourage such regionalism—it is cheaper than foreign aid and not nearly so painful as removing their own protectionism.

The fact is that for a long time to come such regional arrangements as LAFTA, the Central American Market, any African or Asian counterparts (which seem far off at present), or the projected Latin American Common Market now proposed for "completion" in 1985, are of limited economic importance, either to inside or outside countries.

In 1960, for example, nine Latin American countries (since enlarged to eleven) entered into the Treaty of Montevideo creating a Latin American Free Trade Area, that was to have removed tariff and trade barriers by 1972 among the countries concerned. At first, intra-zonal LAFTA trade increased from a mere 6.8% of the countries' total exports to 9.8% in 1965, but in 1966 it dropped back to 8.3%. These figures resemble closely the relationship of all Latin American country exports to each other as compared with their exports as a group to the rest of the world, which also amount to about 10%.[80] It seems clear that even a dramatic increase in trading with each other by less developed countries would still mean that it was overwhelmingly more important for them to develop their trade with developed countries, which, as we have seen, is, and will continue for the foreseable future to be, composed of primary commodity exports.

One reason why the 11-nation LAFTA or indeed a 20-nation Latin American Common Market would have difficulty arriving at what appears to be a modest, and only partly significant, goal of doubling intra-zonal trade, is, as has recently been reported, that "Everyone says they want integration; it means getting into the other fellow's market, but they don't want competition."[81] The large countries, such as Argentina, Brazil, Mexico and Chile have each built automobile, electrical, cement, and other industries behind a high tariff wall, resulting in "parallel, high-cost industrial complexes." It is, of course, quite true that "complementarity" agreements have been discussed, whereby Chile, for example, as the area's largest copper producer, might specialize in selling fabricated wire, cable, and industrial copper products to Argentina, which would then sell Chile automobiles, both at less than either, respectively, could produce them. But they have thus far foundered. Argentina "has copper fabricating plants that entirely supply her own market, and wants only unprocessed copper ingots from Chile." And Chile has allowed a dozen foreign auto assembly plants to start production, "so it doesn't want Argentine vehicles." In this respect, the Central American market, which had few such entrenched local industries, has had a far lesser problem in its early stages.

In addition, the larger and more industrialized countries in the region, such as Argentina, Brazil and Mexico, consider that they have sufficiently large internal markets to "dictate terms to smaller countries," while the medium and smaller countries insist on terms that will help their own industrialization and refuse to be "flooded" by high-cost imports from their big neighbors. A rather piquant by-product of these differences of interest within Latin America is that Mexico has undergone the strange experience of being called the "Colossus of the North"!

There seems little doubt, however, that regional arrangements will continue to be discussed, and even to some extent to develop, however gradually, and with whatever limited effect. For there is only limited relevance in what an experienced World Bank official remarked recently, "What do Peru and Brazil have in common, other than residing in the same continent?"[82] These countries, and others, have something additional in common which is not found in the Charter of the IBRD—the necessity of banding together to restrain, or cajole, or to extract something from, the United States. For the essence of the matter is that regional arrangements are primarily politically motivated groupings. This is said with no tone of disapprobation—the United States needs more restraining and cajoling, and should grant more aid, as great power anywhere needs checks and balances and pushing and pulling; it is simply to express the view that the importance of the "economic integration" effects of regionalism for economic development may not only be small, but in fact may turn out to be less important for such development than the collective bargaining activities associated with regional associations among developing countries, directed toward securing more straight aid.

The benevolent tolerance of, and even assistance to, the efforts of less developed countries to form regional arrangements which has been proffered by the developed countries should be assessed, then, as not being wholly cynical. For to the extent that regional groupings succeed in creating an ambience of greater cohesion, they may be quite welcome to the wiser heads in developed countries, who will welcome some outside assistance, for example, in persuading legislatures to appropriate increased foreign aid. By the same token, however, the economic integration aspects of such cohesion could well be their least important aspect, and in very long run terms, even become quite trying if import substitution were to distort trade patterns unduly to the serious detriment of the exports of the aid-giving outside developed countries.

For developing countries, a greater appearance of cohesion should also be welcome. It could result, for example, in diminishing their current expenditures for expensive military aircraft and similar equipment having no remote relationship to an improvement in living standards.

There is, however, a substantial risk in regionalism among developing countries which has been insufficiently stressed, and may outweigh all of the limited benefits presently foreseeable. For regional arrangements, however difficult to consummate, are a great deal easier to create than are the basic internal economic and social transformations which are required if underdeveloped societies are to modernize themselves. There is a danger, than, that less developed countries, like others similarly situated, will seek to avoid the harder, sharper ascent that is necessary by choosing a path on which movement is visible but which is meandering and quite unclear as to destination. Regionalism, in short, may be still another "soft option" for developing countries, one full of risk.

James Reston has remarked recently[83] that in the light of current incomes, population growth, and existing growth rates, "talk about forming a 'common market' in Latin America seems vaguely unrealistic." He could have said the same about any other region of developing countries. More than that is the trouble. For to the extent that such talk, and even action, serves as a substitute for needed internal transformation, true economic development will be further postponed and rendered even more difficult, and other ugly consequences rendered more likely.

CONCLUSION

The requirements for more rapid economic development of the less developed countries—internal reforms of a character which signify basic transformations in their societies, and drastic reduction of protectionism and much larger amounts of straight economic aid by developed countries in favor of less developed countries—have been attested by a heartening cross section of students of the problem in all countries.

On the other hand, a number of the so-called "trade solutions" to lagging economic development (commodity agreements, preferences, regional arrangements—all the major ones except compensatory financing) are marginal at best in their positive effects upon development, and carry with them serious side effects adverse to a world trading system which aims at the most economic allocation of resources to the benefit of all.

The developing countries might well conserve the energies that they are now employing to secure trade solutions which are so meager in their effective resource-transfer results, and so capable of causing serious difficulties to the rational elements which persist in the existing trading system. They might then devote their energies, collectively, to securing greater amounts of foreign aid (directly and through compensatory financing) and dismantling of protectionism by developed countries, and, individually, to internal societal transformations at home. If they were to shift the direction of their energies in this manner, they would be performing a signal service for themselves and mankind in general.

This is not to say that UNCTAD and the spokesmen for the developing countries have not performed a service these past five years. They have been most valuable. Through collective action, they have focused the attention of the richer nations upon the deepening economic troubles of the poorer nations. That they have done so through an extremely diversified approach, combining requests for more direct aid with a large variety of trade measures, and that they have so far secured limited results, is probably not very important. For this technique has stirred matters up dramatically, perhaps far beyond what more orthodox methods might have succeeded in achieving.

It is now time, however, it may be suggested respectfully, for this leadership to focus upon the most important resource—begetting measures in order to secure the most substantial concrete benefits for all less developed countries. A greater sense of priorities now appears to be in order: much greater direct aid and compensatory financing should be stressed, and the very dubious, divisive, and, in economic terms, small resource—transfer trade items, such as commodity agreements, and preferences, should be dropped or postponed. Regionalism should not be viewed as a substitute for needed internal measures.

It has become almost a cliche to say that in the past two decades the peoples of the underdeveloped world have awakened; that this "revolution of rising expectations" has only begun, and that we will be witness to a rising crescendo of their demand for satisfaction in more just societies than any they have ever experienced. It is nonetheless true. And it takes no Cassandra to see that time is on the side of greater chaos and more misery.

If we, in the developed and underdeveloped countries alike, are serious about seeking to achieve economic development and minimizing chaos and misery, it behooves us to do a great deal more of the right things than presently appear on our agendas.

FOOTNOTES

* When invited to do this paper, I made it clear that it would inevitably reflect a freer trade, high straight-aid viewpoint, and a correspondingly low opinion of trade measures which were disguised aid, and that it would not be an even-handed report, though it would attempt to set out the competing considerations affecting the various issues.

[1] Kenworthy, "Argentina: The Politics of Late Industrialization," 45 Foreign Affairs (April 1967) 462.

[2] Eduardo Frei Montalva, "The Alliance That Lost Its Way", 45 Foreign Affairs (April 1967) 437, 448.

[3] Johnson, ECONOMIC POLICIES TOWARD LESS DEVELOPED COUNTRIES (1967) 44-46. See also Pincus, TRADE, AID, AND DEVELOPMENT (1967). These two books, along with Patterson, DISCRIMINATION IN INTERNATIONAL TRADE, THE POLICY ISSUES 1945-1965 (1966) discuss at great length the issues dealt with in this paper. The description in the text of the requirements of a "modernizing" society has borrowed from Johnson, but selectively and with elements not included by him. Obviously, this text does not describe the particular steps which less developed countries should take, in order of priority, in order to get from where they are to a state of development. So far as I am aware, no one has come forth in recent years with any general blueprint; nor with a series of them for the greatly differing situations amongst the less developed countries.

[4] Johnson, *supra* note 3 at 47.

[5] Statement at 93rd Plenary Meeting, Trade and Development Board of UNCTAD, August 31, 1966 (TD/B/103/Rev. 1, 6 Sept. 1966) 14.

[6] *Supra* note 5 at 15. These percentages are gross figures; there must be subtracted from them, annual increases in population. Hence a 5% figure for Latin America generally must be reduced to about 1-1/2%, because of the 3-1/2% per annum growth in population in that area, in order to reflect growth per capita.

[7] Mikesell, PUBLIC INTERNATIONAL LENDING FOR DEVELOPMENT (1966) is a very good short descriptive analysis of the lending institutions and their policies. A good brief description of various national programs, particularly foreign programs, can be found in Rubin, THE CONSCIENCE OF THE RICH NATIONS (1966) 25-54.

[8] It is next to impossible to secure agreement on what constitutes "aid." The Development Assistance Committee of the OECD's tabulations indicate that total official and private "long-term" flows of financial resources to less developed countries and multilateral agencies (disbursements) amounted to something over $8 billion annually in 1962-1964 (Rubin, *supra,* note 7 at 154-158). However, one must keep in mind that the growing debt burden means that many developing countries are obliged to repay about 50 percent of all new resources transferred (Prebisch, *supra,* note 5 at 5).

[9] Proceedings of the United Nations Conference on Trade and Development: Final Act and Report, UN Document E/Conf. 46/141, Vol. I (1964) 44.

[10] Recently, the Executive Secretary of the United Nations Economic Commission for Asia and the Far East pointed out that the 1% figure was insufficient "in view of higher costs, greater absorptive capacity and greater need in the developing countries as a result of improving technology." He also pointed out that even the 1% figure was not being met and that "we are witnessing the phenomenon of an increasing gap between the developed and the developing countries." N. Y. Times, April 3, 1967.

[11] Washington Post, March 3, 1960; See Metzger, INTERNATIONAL LAW, TRADE AND FINANCE (1962) 130.

[12] *Supra* note 5 at 5, where Mr. Prebisch states that the figure was 0.83 percent in 1961, 0.65 percent in 1964, and 0.69 percent in 1965.

41

13 Isaiah Frank, "New Perspectives on Trade and Development," 45 Foreign Affairs (April 1967) 522. Prof. Frank points out that earnings from exports in the latter half of the 1950's averaged 3% annually. In the 1960-1965 period, however, the rate has been 6% per annum.

14 Some of the conditions imposed upon countries receiving bilateral assistance from the United States are restrictions upon the terms of nationalization of, or breaches of contract concerning, American owned property beyond those imposed by international law; restraints upon trading with Cuba, North Viet-Nam, China, the U.S.S.R. and countries controlled by China or the U.S.S.R.; the requirement that half of all cargoes financed by U.S. governmental funds be shipped in American-flag vessels; and that loans be tied to American purchases. See I Metzger, LAW OF INTERNATIONAL TRADE (1966) 132-137, 247; II Metzger, *op. cit.* 1137-1151, 1154-1157; Rubin, *supra* note 5 at 34-35.

15 See I Metzger, *supra* note 14 at 130-132, for a colloquy during House Banking and Currency Committee hearings on the bill to augment the resources of IDA in 1964, in which U.S. Treasury spokesmen made it clear that countries deprived of U.S. bilateral aid because of "bad" behavior, such as nationalization without prompt compensation in dollars, could not expect to substitute therefor multilateral aid from the IBRD institutions.

16 *Supra* note 8.

17 United Nations Conference on Trade and Development, Basic Documents (1966) 1 (hereinafter referred to as Basic Documents).

18 This "worsening of the terms of trade" argument has been sharply disputed. by many development economists. Johnson, for example, states categorically (*supra,* note 3 at 28-29) that, "[t]he alleged long-run tendency of the terms of trade to move against primary products is not consistent with the empirical evidence, which shows a succession of upward and downward short- and medium-term trends with no clear long-term movement in either direction; nor are the theoretical explanations presented to support it logically satisfactory...nevertheless, the alleged adverse trend of the terms of trade of primary products is the basis of the recommendations for trade policy in this field."

19 Basic Documents 4-5.

20 Basic Documents 45-56.

21 Johnson, *supra* note 3 at 136.

22 U.S. Dept. of State Pub. No. 3206 (1948).

23 61 Stat. 716 (1947), 19 U.S.C. Sec. 1201 (1958).

24 Chapter V of the ITO Charter, Art. 46 (reprinted in I Metzger, *supra* note 14, at 1486). Since the demise of the ITO Charter there has been no general international agreement relating to cartels, though the EEC and the Coal and Steel Community treaties legislate against them.

25 Metzger, "Inter-governmental Commodity Agreements: The Actuality," in II Metzger, *supra* note 14, at 1202, 1210.

26 Rowe, PRIMARY COMMODITIES IN INTERNATIONAL TRADE (1965) 121.

27 Rowe, *supra* note 26, at 120-155, contains a very good summary of the commodity control schemes as they evolved in this century until 1945. Earlier monographs were Knorr, TIN UNDER CONTROL (1945), Wickizer, TEA UNDER INTERNATIONAL REGULATION (1944), and Bauer, THE RUBBER INDUSTRY (1948).

28 Rowe, *supra* note 26 at 141, 143.

29 Rowe, *supra* note 26 at 157.

30 Chapter VI, *supra* note 22, Article 55.

31 *Supra* note 30, Articles 60, 62, 63, 64 and 65.

32 Rowe, *supra* note 26 at 157.

33 Rowe, *supra* note 26 at 213-214.

42

34 Rowe, *supra* note 26 at 209.

35 See Mikesell, "Commodity Agreements and Aid to Developing Countries," 28 Law & Contemp. Prob. 294 (1963); Mikesell, "International Commodity Stabilization Schemes and the Export Problems of Developing Countries", 1962 Proceedings American Economic Association 75.

36 Basic Documents 34 (Final Act UNCTAD Conf. 1964); Frank, *supra* note 13 at 526; a note by the UNCTAD Secretariat, "The Development of an International Commodity Policy", TD/B/C. 1/26, Oct. 26, 1966 at p. 3 makes this quite explicit, stating that "the fundamental objective of inter-governmental co-operation in the field of primary commodity trade should be to act on market forces in such a way as to facilitate the maximization of export income ... commodity policy needs to be directed towards achieving the maximum possible level of earnings from exports of the primary products of the developing countries."

37 Rowe, *supra* note 26 at 215.

38 See Rowe, *supra* note 26 at 124-126 for a brief summary of these schemes; rubber and copper production, respectively in 1925 and 1926 were deliberately restrained in order to raise prices precipitately, resulting in huge monopolistic profits.

39 Rowe, *supra* note 26 at 216.

40 Frank, *supra* note 13 at 528-529; Pincus, *supra* note 3 at 267-284.

41 "The Development of an International Commodity Policy", *supra* note 36 at p. 4.

42 Frank, *supra* note 13 at 526-527.

43 Rowe, *supra* note 26 at 214.

44 Prebisch, *supra* note 5 at 7-8; see also "The Development of an International Commodity Policy", *supra* note 36 at 38-40.

45 "Compensatory Financing of Export Fluctuations," A Report by the International Monetary Fund (Feb. 1963).

46 "Compensatory Financing of Export Fluctuations", A Second Report by the International Monetary Fund (Sept. 1966).

47 United Nations, International Compensation for Fluctuations in Commodity Trade (Report by a Committee of Experts, E/CN. 13/40, N. Y. 1961).

48 Organization of American States, Final Report of the Group of Experts on the Stabilization of Export Receipts (Washington D.C. 1962).

49 1963 IMF Report 3-4.

50 1963 IMF Report 23-26.

51 Frank, *supra* note 13 at 530.

52 1966 IMF Second Report 30-32.

53 1966 IMF Second Report 30.

54 Frank, *supra* note 13 at 530.

55 "Supplementary Financial Measures" (I. B. R. D. 1965) at 6-7 spells out the "general premises" upon which the Scheme on supplementary finance is based. The paragraph in the text is a summary of the Bank's report in this respect.

56 UNCTAD Monthly Bulletin No. 9, March 1967 summarized the February 1967 session in the manner described in the text.

57 Mikesell, "International Commodity Stabilization Schemes and the Export Problems of Developing Countries," 1962 Proceedings American Economic Assocciation 75, 82.

58 The literature on preferences is large and growing. Some representative studies and discussions are found in Johnson, *supra* note 3 at Chapter VI, 163-211; Pincus, *supra* note 3 at Chapter 6, 177-232; Patterson, *supra* note 3 at Chapter VII, 323-384; "The Question of the Granting and Extension of Prefer-

ences in Favour of Developing Countries," report by Secretary-General of UNCTAD to Trade and Development Board Committee on Manufactures, TD/B/C.2/AC.1/2/Rev. 1, July 12, 1966; and "Preferences and other Policy Measures to Stimulate Exports of the Less Developed Countries," a study by the GATT Secretariat (Trade Intelligence Paper No. 7, July 1966).

59 Prior to the U.S.-German treaty of 1923, the U.S. had from the beginnings of the republic adhered to "conditional" most-favored-nation treatment, where-under advantages accrue to a 3d country only on payment therefor of compensation equivalent to that paid by the 2d country. For materials illustrating the policy considerations involved in the shift to the unconditional form, see 1 Foreign Relations of the United States 1923, 121-131 (1938); 2 Foreign Relations of the United States 1924, 183-192 (1939). See also Culbertson, RECIPROCITY 167-170, 238-279 (1937); Excerpt, Staff Papers, Commission on Foreign Economic Policy of U.S. (1954) 255-264, 269-276, reprinted in I Metzger, *supra* note 14 at 621-646.

60 48 Stat. 944 (1934), as amended, 69 Stat. 164 (1955), 19 U.S.C. Sec. 1351 (1958); Sec. 251, Trade Expansion Act of 1962. Beginning in 1951 this requirement that trade agreement concessions must be applied to products of all foreign countries was withdrawn as to goods from the U.S.S.R., Communist China, and countries dominated or controlled by them, which were thenceforth required to pay statutory rates as unreduced by concessions. In addition, beginning in 1934, authority has been granted to suspend this requirement when another country has discriminated against American goods; in the 1962 Act this authority was expanded to cover unreasonable or unjustifiable discriminations. See Metzger, TRADE AGREEMENTS AND THE KENNEDY ROUND (1964) 30-37.

61 The new Part IV of GATT specifically recognizes the need for expanded export earnings for developing countries and obliges developed countries to "accord high priority" to the reduction and elimination of barriers thereto and to refrain from introducing new ones; see I Metzger, *supra* note 14 at 589, 591-2 for text of the new Part. Unfortunately, this seems to have had little influence upon the action of developed countries in restraining imports of textile manufactures from developing countries. See text accompanying note 67, *infra*.

62 Johnson, *supra*, note 3 at 114.

63 *Ibid.*

64 This is the argument that protection of an infant industry in its years of early development enables it to grow in a sheltered market to a point where its development can assure its survival after tariff barriers come down. The landscape in all countries seems to be dotted, however, by 60, 80 or even 150 year old "infants". Moreover, recently the infant-industry argument has turned to the "infant-economy" argument in respect of the necessity for and duration of preferences, which of course means that the infant-industry argument becomes more of a slogan than an analogy.

65 Frank, *supra* note 13 at 532.

66 "Effective" tariffs are generally higher than "nominal" rates due to the admission into developed countries of raw materials and semi-finished goods at lower rates than finished goods. This means that there is a relatively higher tariff on the act of manufacturing in developing countries than is revealed in the rate on the manufactured import itself. See Johnson, *supra*, note 3, at 96-101; Frank, *supra*, note 13 at 532-33.

67 Frank, *supra* note 13 at 534.

68 Pincus, *supra* note 3 at 198-199.

69 It is not clear at this writing that there will be important exceptions, so far as tariff reductions for products of interest to developing countries are concerned, at the Kennedy Round negotiations. Of course, tariff reductions on cotton textiles will have no effect upon the volume of developing countries' textiles exports to developed countries so long as the long-term cotton textile arrangement remains in force.

[70] Prebisch, *supra* note 5 at 10. Mr. Prebisch specifically has opposed the "sectional" or "vertical" preference idea, such as the EEC's preferences for imports from former colonial African countries, because they would take the world "further and further away from the principle of the most-favored-nation clause and the principle of multi-lateral trade." Noting that these kinds of "vertical" systems "would promote other similar systems in the world," and that this is "a dangerous path," he ruefully adds, "there are clear signs that this is the path we have embarked on."

[71] European Community, the Bulletin of the EEC, reported in No. 99, December 1966-January 1967, p. 9, that the 1966 meeting of the countries forming the Yaoundé Convention, which associates 18 African and Malagasy states with the EEC, disclosed that the associate states' exports to the EEC had actually dropped slightly between 1964 and 1965 (from $1,150 million to $1,146 million). In view of this, one new step favored by the African states was "[EEC] levies on certain tropical imports from non-associated countries, at least when the Yaoundé asociates could supply the products."!

[72] Johnson, *supra* note 3 at 196; Patterson, *supra* note 3 at 340, 364-369.

[73] Johnson, *supra* note 3 at 197-198.

[74] *Ibid.*

[75] *Ibid.*

[76] *Id.*

[77] See Patterson, *supra* note 3 at 145-155 for an examination of the rationale for regional arrangements amongst developing countries.

[78] See Metzger, "Regional Markets and International Law," *supra* note 11 at 89, 92-93, 96-98.

[78a] In the current Kennedy Round negotiations, the EEC's Common Agricultural Policy, which is autarchic in nature, making "residual suppliers" out of outside suppliers of temperate products such as grains, has become a major source of contention. See February 20, 1967, Cong. Rec. (Daily ed.) H1538. For a good descriptive analysis of the Common Agricultural Policy, see Dam, "The European Common Market in Agriculture," 67 Col. L. R. 209 (1967); Riesenfeld, "Common Market for Agricultural Products and Common Agricultural Policy in the European Economic Community," 1965 U. Ill. L. F. 658.

[79] Johnson uses the term "soft option" to describe the choice of developed countries to proffer financial aid to less developed countries rather than to offer reductions in domestic protectionism against imports from developing countries. See Johnson, *supra,* note 3 at 3.

[80] The figures are drawn from an excellent dispatch in the N. Y. Times, April 2, 1967, by Juan de Onis, "The Goal is a Latin Market." See also his fine article on the problems of a Latin American Common Market in N. Y. Times, April 10, 1967.

[81] *Ibid.*

[82] James Reston makes the same point in the New York Times, April 7, 1967, "Buenos Aires, The Lost Continent," where he writes that "Buenos Aires is closer to Europe in spirit than to Caracas or Mexico City. It costs less to ship heavy produce from Antwerp to Buenos Aires than from Santiago in Chile to Buenos Aires. The spectacular range of the Andes is a greater barrier between the Atlantic and Pacific nations of the hemisphere than the two oceans themselves."

[83] New York Times, April 5, 1947, "Rio de Janeiro: The Agony of Latin America."

PART TWO

THE FORUM PROCEEDINGS

The Eleventh Hammarskjöld Forum was held on Tuesday, April 25, 1967, at the House of The Association of the Bar of the City of New York, 42 West 44th Street, New York, New York.

CHAIRMAN JOHN CAREY: Mr. President, distinguished guests, ladies and gentlemen.

First, we want to bid a warm welcome to the two organizations with whose cooperation our Committee has organized this forum. They are the United Nations Association and the United States Council of the International Chamber of Commerce.

Next I want to thank the members of our Committee, as well as Mr. Paul DeWitt, and the other people on the staff of The Association of the Bar of the City of New York. Our particular thanks are due to Professor Stanley D. Metzger, the author of the outstanding working paper which you have received in the mail, or can pick up outside this room. The working paper contains a detailed bibliography compiled by Mr. Anthony Grech of The Association.

The committee which has organized this eleventh in the series of Hammarskjöld Forums bears the name of the Special Committee on the Lawyer's Role in the Search for Peace. Why does a committee with a name stressing the search for peace believe that trade among "have" and and "have-not" nations is a subject which comes within its scope? Why do we feel that trade among the rich and poor members of the international community is a problem in peacekeeping like the crises in Berlin, the Congo, Cuba, Panama and the Dominican Republic, which are some of the subjects dealt with in previous Hammarskjöld Forums?

The answer is that we have heard very prominent people declare that future world peace depends upon the solution of the more serious economic problems. The Secretary Gen-

49

eral of the United Nations said last spring that the "widening gulf between the 'haves' and the 'have-nots' constitutes a more serious threat to international peace and security than any other rifts, either ideological or racial." Last summer he said, "I believe that the economic problems, ultimately, if there are no solutions, are more explosive than the political problems." Again last summer U Thant declared that "the growing gap between the developed and less developed countries, between the rich and the poor, the haves and the have-nots, in the world ... is, indeed, the most crucial and the most challenging long-term struggle of this century. For just as the internal stability of the advanced nations has proved to rest on narrowing the gap between the rich and the poor, so will the future stability of the relations between nations and of peace itself." This is the opinion of U Thant.

Now hear what Pope Paul said last month in his Encyclical "Populorum Progressio": "The same duty of solidarity that rests on individuals exists also for nations: 'Advanced nations have a very heavy obligation to help the developing peoples.' We must repeat once more that the superfluous wealth of rich countries should be placed at the service of poor nations, the rule which up to now held good for the benefit of those nearest to us, must today be applied to all the needy of this world. Besides, the rich will be the first to benefit as a result. Otherwise their continued greed will certainly call down upon them the judgment of God and the wrath of the poor, with consequences no one can foretell."

The Pope stated that, "as a result of technical progress, the value of manufactured goods is rapidly increasing and they can always find an adequate market. On the other hand, raw materials produced by underdeveloped countries are subject to wide and sudden fluctuations in price, a state of affairs far removed from the progressively increasing value of industrial products. As a result, nations whose industrialization is limited are faced with serious difficulties when they have to rely on their exports to balance their economy and to carry out their plans for development. The poor nations remain ever poor while the rich ones become still richer. In other words," said the Pope, "the rule of free trade, taken by itself, is no longer able to govern international relations."

The Pope continued: "What was true of the just wage for the individual is also true of international contracts: An economy of exchange can no longer be based solely on the law of free competition, a law which, in its turn, too often creates an economic dictatorship. Freedom of trade is fair only if it is subject to the demands of social justice."

Now, in the light of these opinions relating the prosperity gap among nations to the keeping of the peace, our Committee believes that the lawyer's role in solving this set of problems should be examined. For this purpose we are fortunate in having with us this evening two lawyers who are also highly trained in economics and an economist with many years of experience in banking and government and in the development of international institutions for coping with economic problems.

Our first speaker, Dr. Raúl Prebisch, was born in Argentina. He graduated from the University of Buenos Aires with a degree in economics and was a professor of political economy in that university from 1925 until 1948. During the early part of this period he was Deputy Director of the Department of Statistics in Argentina, followed by service as Director of Economic Research for the National Bank of Argentina. He was Under Secretary of Finance from 1930 to 1932; and Advisor to the Ministers of Finance and Agriculture from 1933 to 1935. From 1935 to 1943, he was the organizer and first Director General of the Central Bank of the Republic of Argentina.

In 1948 Dr. Prebisch joined the Secretariat of the United Nations Economic Commission for Latin America, and was its Executive Secretary from 1950 to 1963. He is an honorary member of the faculty of universities not only in Argentina, but also in Chile, Bolivia and Peru, and has received an honorary doctorate from the University of the Andes in Colombia, as well as from Columbia University here in New York.

Since 1964 Dr. Prebisch has been connected with the UN Conference on Trade and Development, which has been established as a permanent organ of the General Assembly. Dr. Prebisch is the Secretary-General of this relatively new member of the UN family of organizations, popularly known as UNCTAD because of its initials. Since UNCTAD has its seat in Geneva, we are especially fortunate in having with us this evening Dr. Raúl Prebisch.

DR. RAÚL PREBISCH: Mr. Chairman, ladies and gentlemen.

When my admired friend Richard Gardner invited me on behalf of The Association to speak tonight, I did not hesitate to accept this very kind invitation, as I do not like to lose any opportunity to appear before a distinguished audience in order to explain the problems confronting this new organization of the United Nations.

I do not need to underline the paramount importance of the problems that developing countries and the world as a whole are facing now after the very timely quotations that Mr. Carey has just presented to you, the quotation of U Thant in which he calls the attention of the world to the growing seriousness of the problem of developing countries, the growing gap between the developed world and the developing world, and the quotation of His Holiness the Pope in this already historical document where he presents with great vigor and clarity the responsibilities of the world vis-a-vis the problems of the developing countries.

What are the reasons for this increasing gap between the developed countries and the developing countries? It is not only a gap in income; there is also a very serious development in relation to trade. Let us remember that in the last fifteen years the proportion of trade of developing countries within total world trade has been consistently declining. In the early fifties, the proportion of trade corresponding to developing countries was 27 percent of world trade, excluding oil. Today it is only about 16 percent.

This is a very important fact that reveals one of the greatest obstacles interfering with the process of economic development of the developing nations. This relative deterioration of their share of trade is one of the explanations why the very modest target of 5 percent minimum growth per year for the the developing world, a target established by the General Assembly of the United Nations when it proclaimed the Development Decade, has not been fulfilled. Indeed, their average rate of growth in the last few years has not surpassed the figure of 4.5 percent, which is very low if one takes into consideration the very high rate of population growth. It means that per capita income in developing countries is growing very, very slowly with tremendous political and social consequences.

Tonight I will not enter into a full explanation of the complexities of the problem. There is no time to present to you the combination of all external and internal factors that are interfering with the process of growth in developing countries. I will deal only with the main trade factors involved, but not overlooking, of course, that the need for a transformation of the economic and social structure of developing countries and for the transformation of attitudes in both developed and developing countries is a factor of considerable importance in the process of growth. Indeed, the best and most enlightened policy of international cooperation is bound to fail if developing countries do not fulfill their very serious responsibility of introducing fundamental reforms in their internal economic and social structure. On the other hand, these internal self-help efforts will not go very far if they are not supplemented by appropriate and opportune external assistance, particularly in the trade field.

Why is the proportion of trade of developing countries deteriorating in the impressive way that I have pointed out? There are a number of explanations. First, there is the well known fact that when income increases at such a fast rate as it has recently in developed countries, the demand there for primary goods, especially for imports of primary goods, tends to grow at a very sluggish pace, as compared to the demand for manufactured products. Secondly, there are various technological factors involved. No doubt you are aware, for instance, of the various technological changes whereby natural products are being substituted by synthetics and other artificial products.

Last, but not least, we must keep in mind the highly protectionist policy prevailing in a number of important developed countries which adversely affects the exports of the developing world. Perhaps the most conspicuous example of this policy and of the damaging effects it has on developing countries is the case of sugar. Almost every important industrial country in the world is producing sugar at a very high cost and protecting this local production to the detriment of the low-cost produced sugar exports of the developing countries. This is creating a tremendous problem for the latter countries, a tremendous problem that has to be solved in some way.

This complexity of factors explains why exports of primary goods from developing countries are growing at a very sluggish rate, except in the case of such products as petroleum. But, in general, there is a very slow rate of growth in their traditional exports. In contrast, the more the developing countries try to accelerate their rate of economic growth, the more they need to import capital goods, intermediate goods and consumer goods, so that we are facing a growing disparity between the tendency for their exports to increase very slowly on the one hand, while on the other, their import requirements are expanding at a very accelerated pace.

This tendency towards external imbalance has been called, during the first UNCTAD conference, the "trade gap" of developing countries. I am sure you all understand very well, ladies and gentlemen, that a country cannot grow adequately if faced with a continuous external imbalance. It has to be stopped, as otherwise economic growth will stop. One of the most important policy objectives of this new organization of the United Nations is to help correct this tendency towards external imbalance which is interfering with the process of economic growth of the developing world. Here is where trade measures are of paramount importance: how to correct this tendency towards imbalance; how to narrow gradually the presently widening gap between the slow movement of traditional exports and the rapid rise of imports in developing countries.

Two fundamental trade measures are necessary. The first is import substitution. If developing countries cannot obtain additional financial resources, particularly in the way of export earnings, to cover their growing import needs, they can substitute imports by internal production. But this is by no means an easy process for the developing countries. If they attempt to substitute imports of industrial goods in very narrow and easily saturated national markets, as is the prevailing case in developing countries, they often enter into a very costly and inefficient process of industrialization. Take the case of the Latin American countries which had been trying to industrialize in twenty almost watertight compartments, with every country trying to produce everything and therefore far too frequently doing so under very inefficient conditions, at very high cost, and with very little room for adequate competition.

Competition is an essential factor for healthy industrial growth anywhere. Indeed, you know very well, ladies and gentlemen, that socialist countries are now increasingly aware of the need to introduce internal and external competition in their economy as a factor for efficiency. The same holds true in Latin America as well as in other developing regions of the world where the process of industrialization has made some advances.

How then to avoid this inefficient type of industrialization in the developing world? One very important way is by the formation of common markets or free trade areas. By enlarging the national markets and merging national markets into wider, broader regional or sub-regional markets. This new process has already started in the developing world and, in this respect, I cannot refrain today from expressing my views as to the importance of the meeting of Presidents recently held in Punta del Este. At this meeting, the Latin American Presidents attending have for the first time taken the historical decision to form a Latin American Common Market by the gradual merging of the Central American Common Market with the Free Trade Association formed in 1960 by a group of important countries of Latin America. The Presidents have taken this decision and they have requested experts to discuss and prepare a series of practical formulas which would enable the formation of a regional common market by 1970 and its full operation by 1985——15 years is not too long a time for this very difficult enterprise.

It is highly important, in my view, that the machinery to achieve the objectives of the Latin American Common Market has been started. And what President Johnson declared at that meeting is of no lesser importance. I consider his speech very constructive and I do not hesitate to say so after weighing it very carefully in relation to what should be done in Latin America itself.

First, President Johnson has committed the full support of the United States to the establishment of the Latin American Common Market. Of course, the Latin American Common Market is something that the Latin Americans have to create with their own hands, according to their own views and conception of the matter. But it is essential, as it was in Europe, to have the cooperation of important industrial countries, and in this particular case, the cooperation of the United States, without excluding, of course, the cooperation of other developed countries. I attach great importance to this question. On the one hand the Latin American decision, and on the other hand, the United States commitment to support this Latin American initiative.

But there is another aspect in President Johnson's speech to which I would like to call your attention, because it responds to the second subject that I was going to present to you. In addition to this collective type effort on the part of developing countries to facilitate their import substitution process within a common market, it is essential, in order to bridge their trade gap, that exports of manufactures from developing countries to developed countries increase substantially. In my view there is no possibility of adequately accelerating the rate of growth of developing countries if appropriate measures are not taken to promote much greater exports from them in the field of manufacturing.

As no doubt Professor Gardner recalls very well—this was one of the central points discussed in the First UNCTAD Conference in Geneva in 1964—developing countries have insistently requested from developed countries a preferential policy that would facilitate their exports of manufactures and semi-manufactures to the industrial centres of the world. While it is true that in 1964 a number of industrial countries supported this idea, the United States was reluctant to enter into any commitment in this respect due to the fact that, among other reasons, this country continued to adhere strongly to the most-favoured-nation clause. Well, one of the most significant steps taken at the recent Presidential meeting in Punta del Este was the declaration made by President Johnson to the effect that his government is aware of the need to introduce changes in the American trade policy, and that it is now willing and prepared to explore together with other industrial countries the possibility of establishing a system of generalized preferences for the exports of manufactures and semi-manufactures from the developing nations.

This is a declaration of far-reaching significance, not only for Latin America, but for the whole of the developing world because one of the most interesting aspects is that the United States has resisted wisely the temptation to organize a system of hemispheric preferences. On the contrary, President Johnson has insisted that preferences should be given to all developing countries without dividing the world into vertical North-South zones of influence involving certain big powers and certain developing regions. This is highly important, because we were running the risk that the policy of vertical preferences that the European Common Market is following in Africa could lead other regions of the developing world to adopt a similar policy. Therefore, I think that one of the greatest merits and most important aspects of President Johnson's declaration is precisely that he spoke of a system of preferences for all developing nations, which is the only way to avoid the division of the world into zones of influence.

Now, what of the most-favoured-nation clause? Wouldn't a general preferential system mean a new departure from the principle of the most-favoured-nation clause? I myself consider this principle, as well as the related principle of multilateral trade, to be among the greatest trade policy achievements of the 19th century, and they still have great validity.

Here, let me enter very briefly into some legal aspects of international trade. The most-favoured-nation principle entails a certain legal order in world trade and seeks to assure equal terms of competition. Why then are we advocating a preferential policy that implies a departure from this principle? Well, not because there are already a number of other departures from this principle. There was recently such a departure, for example, when the United States and Canada signed a pact in relation to motor cars. There was certainly a tremendous departure from this prin-

58

ciple when the European Common Market was established, as it allows discrimination vis-a-vis other countries. This meant a departure from a rigid interpretation of the most-favoured-nation clause.

Nevertheless I do think that the departure from this principle that was allowed to form the European Common Market was and is a way to assure in the world another order of things within which the most-favoured-nation clause may itself acquire a new meaning and vitality, because modern technology demands big economic spaces and the need to facilitate and expedite the advance of technology was and is a factor of considerable importance in the formation of the European Common Market, as in the formation of the Latin American Common Market and other common markets and free trade areas, or special arrangements in other parts of the world.

It is precisely the formation of the European Common Market which has facilitated in many ways lowering of tariffs in the developed world. Without the creation of the European Common Market, the trade policy liberalization of the last fifteen years and the new advance that this policy of liberalization will now have, notwithstanding all the difficulties encountered in the Kennedy Round, might not have happened at all. And I hope that the formation of the Latin American Common Market will also be conducive in the course of time to a lowering of the external tariff of Latin American countries vis-a-vis the rest of the world.

After all, what are the preferences involved? As in the case of the formation of common markets, the preferential system that the developing nations envisage for their industrial exports is a means of strengthening the industrial structure, as well as a means of bridging their trade gap. We are not asking for preferences for a very long time but for a temporary period only, and this was made very clear in the speech of President Johnson at Punta del Este. It is, if you wish, a new presentation of the fairly old and famous infant-industry argument so often used to promote national industrial development, but its objective now would not be to develop industry for internal consumption only, but also to develop industry outwardly, with a view to greatly increasing exports of manufactures and, thereby, of trade in general.

When the industrial structure of developing countries is improved and strengthened through the operation of common markets and a preferential policy, then developing countries could play a very efficient role in further liberalizing world trade. Then and only then could we put on a truly solid basis in the developing world the principle of the most-favoured-nation clause. Let us not forget, ladies and gentlemen, that the break-down of the world trade system in the thirties, the numerous violations of the law of trade, was not the result of an international movement; it was the consequence of the disruption of world trade itself.

If the proportion of trade of the developing world continues to deteriorate within the global trade picture, we are bound to see the destruction of what remains of the most-favoured-nation clause and of the multilateral trade system in the developing world. In my view, the only way to strengthen the basis for the restoration in the whole world of this sound principle of trade, is to take more effective measures in relation to developing countries, to help them promote their exports of manufactures and semi-manufactures, and to promote and support the attempts in every developing region of the world, to integrate and to form common markets.

Mr. Chairman, ladies and gentlemen, I think that I have arrived at the end of my time limit. I would have liked to comment on aid and trade, and I hope Professor Metzger will speak about this subject. I am afraid that we may differ perhaps in this aspect. I do not advocate trade versus aid, or aid versus trade, but trade and aid. Trade and aid have their respective roles. I do not think that only trade will solve the problem of development, nor that aid alone can resolve it. What is required is a wise combination of both trade and aid.

Thank you, ladies and gentlemen.

CHAIRMAN CAREY: Dr. Prebisch, thank you very much indeed for giving us the privilege of hearing you explain so clearly these most vital points, and we look forward to your further comments later on in the more informal portion of the program.

Introducing our next speaker is a special pleasure because he and his family have been such close friends of my family and myself ever since he and I met as colleagues in the same law firm. Having heard many of his witty introductions of other people, I realize it is not possible to equal the standard he sets in this regard. For example, I have heard him introduce someone named Gold with a reference to the gold standard. The best I can do to try to equal that is to say that this is one Gardner with whom it is an honor and a joy to labor in the same vineyard. Actually in his case there is so much notable biography to relate that it would be wrong to waste time on frivolities.

Mr. Gardner, now Henry L. Moses Professor of Law and International Organization at Columbia University, received in 1948 his undergraduate degree in economics, magna cum laude, at Harvard, where he was Phi Beta Kappa. After obtaining an L.L.B. three years later at Yale, where he was Note Editor of the Law Journal, he went to Oxford as a Rhodes Scholar and there earned a Ph. D. in economics in 1954. His unusual double training in the two fields of law and economics has been supplemented by experience as a correspondent associated with the United Press, several years of law practice here in New York, more than four years on the firing line in Washington as Deputy Assistant Secretary of State for International Organization Affairs, and a number of years as a law teacher both in his home university of Columbia, and also as a visiting pro-

61

fessor at the University of Istanbul. He is the author of many articles and of four books, the newest of which will be published in the fall under the title "Economic Development and International Organizations," co-edited with Professor Max Milliken of M.I.T.

Professor Gardner has been in the forefront in representing the United States at economic conferences held in the past several years. He was vice chairman of the U.S. delegation to the UN Conference on Trade and Development in 1964, and the U.S. representative in the committee which set up conciliation procedures within UNCTAD. I am told that in the spring of 1964 he spent most of his time at Dr. Prebisch's apartment, where, in a very smoke-filled room, some important decisions were hammered out. He has also served a number of times as a member of the U.S. delegation to the General Assembly, was a Senior Advisor to Ambassador Goldberg at the 1965 and 1966 General Assembly sessions, and continues to serve as a member of the Department of State's Advisory Committee on International Organization.

Professor Richard Gardner.

PROFESSOR RICHARD N. GARDNER: Thank you, Mr. Chairman.

ORGANIZATIONAL PROBLEMS

In a moment I shall suggest a five-point program to escalate the international war on poverty. Before doing so, however, let me mention two institutional questions which deserve the attention of lawyers as well as economists and specialists in international organization.

The first of these questions might be formulated as "voting machine versus consensus."

It has not escaped your attention, I am sure, that the expansion of membership of the UN has posed the very difficult problem of how decisions are to be taken in the

UN and its related bodies, both on peacekeeping and economic matters. A two-thirds majority can now be mustered in the General Assembly or UNCTAD by countries paying only five percent of the total budget and representing only ten percent of the population of the membership.

At the UNCTAD Conference, some resolutions were voted by two-thirds majorities which represented less than one-third of world trade—over the opposition of a minority of countries which represented more than two-thirds of world trade. Many of us at the Conference were concerned about this, and we raised the question whether this was a sensible way to proceed. Economic questions between nations, we argued, must be settled by negotiation—not legislation. And we suggested some procedures to assure that resolutions were adopted on the basis of a consensus sufficient to assure that the resolutions would be carried out.

Some representatives of the less developed countries were reluctant to accept such procedures. One of them explained his position as follows: "Those in possession must be relieved of their possessions. There are only two ways to do this—by force or by votes. We don't have the force, but we do have the votes. And now you are trying to take away our votes!"

I am happy to say that a wiser view finally prevailed. For this Dr. Prebisch deserves a very large measure of credit. Under his leadership we worked out a conciliation procedure designed to substitute conciliation for voting on disagreed questions. This procedure is in the interests of both "have" and "have not" nations. It is obviously of little value for the less developed countries to vote recommendations over the opposition of the developed countries when those recommendations call for action by the developed countries and the defeated minority has no intention of taking such action; what is wanted, after all, is not voting, but results.

It has been a source of great satisfaction that since the UNCTAD Conference in 1964 the Trade Board and its committees have in fact operated by consensus. The conciliation machinery has never been formally invoked, but it has served as a silent deterrent. Because *de jure* conciliation is possible, *de facto* conciliation has become standard practice.

The second organizational question might be posed as "fragmentation versus consolidation." Here there is somewhat less room for optimism than on the first question.

We have in the United Nations a vast array of economic machinery. There are the General Assembly and the Economic and Social Council. There is the Headquarters Secretariat. There are special programs like the UN Development Program and the UN Children's Fund. There are four Regional Economic Commissions. There are 14 Specialized and Affiliated Agencies. We have UNCTAD and the new UN Industrial Development Organization (UNIDO). And, of course, we have the GATT, not formally part of the UN but cooperating with it.

Alexander the Great is reputed to have said, "I am dying with the aid of too many physicians." The less developed countries might make the same complaint. There are too many physicians, holding too many meetings, writing too many reports, and giving advice which is often contradictory.

The Secretary-General of the UN recently called attention to the special problems created by UNCTAD and UNIDO: "The creation of autonomous units within the Secretariat and therefore under my jurisdiction as chief administrative officer raises serious questions of organizational authority and responsibility. Such a trend is not altogether consistent with the concept of a unified Secretariat working as a team towards the accomplishment of the main goals of the organization. On the contrary, it may tend to have the adverse effect of pitting one segment of the Secretariat against the other in competition for the necessary financial and political support of its own work programs."

The problem here is not just one of budgetary economy. If we can deal more effectively with the problems of development with an additional ten million dollars, it is obviously worth it. But more institutions do not always add up to greater effectiveness.

On the contrary, there is a tendency to go at problems in a piecemeal fashion. Take the important question of expanding the manufactured exports of the less developed countries. You have the ILO training workers and management in industrial establishments. You have UNIDO assisting in the development of industry. You have GATT and UNCTAD concerned with the promotion of exports.

What is needed is an inter-related and inter-disciplinary attack on problems of this kind. They cannot be artificially segregated in accordance with the separate bureaucratic responsibilities. For example, the decision on what industry to establish is integrally related to the question of its export prospects.

This is a great challenge to the United Nations—to get the multiplicity of agencies to work together effectively. Efforts are now underway in this direction, but they are in the nature of self-coordination by largely autonomous bodies. If these efforts prove inadequate to the task, a major constitutional reform will be required to enable the UN system to play its full part in the international war on poverty. One possibility would be the creation of a Director-General for Economic Affairs, who would have authority over some or all of the multifarious programs that have hitherto been independent.

A PROGRAM OF ACTION

Let us turn now from the organizational to the policy questions. What must be done by national governments to make greater progress in the international war on poverty? I believe a new level of effort is needed in at least five main areas.

John F. Kennedy once said, "If we cannot help the many who are poor, we cannot save the few who are rich." If this is true, and surely it is, then we are in deep trouble. For the international war on poverty is now being lost. The time has come for escalation. This is one war in which there is no substitute for victory.

In this decade of the 1960s—a decade hopefully designated as the "Decade of Development" by the United Nations—the average annual increase in gross national product of the poor countries has been little more than 4 percent. With rates of population growth in most countries averaging 2 or 3 percent, there has been only a 1 or 2 percent average annual increase in individual living standards. Indeed, the average rate of increase in per capita income in the 1960s has actually been lower than in the decade of the 1950s.

To turn the tide, we need new forms of international cooperation and an entirely new level of effort on the part of *both* developed and less developed countries. The efforts of rich and poor countries alike are now grossly inadequate when measured against the problem to be solved—the achievement of standards of living in the less developed countries compatible with minimum human dignity.

I. TRADE

For much too long the United States and other industrial countries have tended to conduct their aid and trade policies in separate compartments. We have had an aid policy directed toward the less developed countries and a trade policy directed mainly toward other industrialized countries. The time has come to fashion a trade policy fully equal to our aid objectives. Let us not forget that the less developed countries earn at least three times as much foreign exchange from exports as they do from foreign aid.

The United States, in association with as many other industrialized countries as possible, should put into effect, in stages over the next 20 years, a policy of one-way free trade in favor of the less developed countries. In other words, our protection on both manufactured and primary product imports from these countries should be reduced to zero, without asking for reciprocity from the less developed countries in return. While the policy would be implemented gradually over a period of twenty years, a commitment to this objective should be taken *now*.

The key to progress in difficult matters of this kind is gradualism related to a realistic target date. Our domestic civil rights problem provides an analogy. When, following the Supreme Court's decision of 1954, some proposed desegregating schools in the South one grade at a time—beginning with the first grade and letting white and colored children grow up together, this was denounced as too slow. Yet if such a plan had been implemented the schools would be fully integrated today.

Some first steps in the gradual implementation of a one-way free trade policy would include:

—liberalization and then elimination of the long-term cotton textile agreement;

—elimination of tariffs on products of tropical agriculture and forestry, without the limitations currently imposed in the Trade Expansion Act (i.e., without requiring similar action from the Common Market and without requiring that the products not be produced in the U.S. in significant quantities);

—reduction of tariffs on processed industrial materials so as to eliminate "tariff escalation by stages of production"—a feature of our tariff structure which discourages less developed countries from processing their own raw materials.

Authority for these last two actions, and perhaps others, might be embodied in a new Trade for Economic Develop-

67

ment Act in which Congress would explicitly recognize the contribution of a freer trade policy toward the economic development of the less developed countries.

Of course, the most severe restrictions against the exports of the less developed countries do not take the form of tariffs. The primary product exports which account for 85 to 90 percent of the exports of less developed countries are mainly held back by non-tariff barriers maintained by the United States and other countries. Professor Harry Johnson has estimated as follows the losses in export earnings of the less developed countries resulting from such policies: agricultural protectionism in developed countries —$2 billion, U.S. sugar quotas—$357-525 million; European duties and excises on coffee, cocoa and bananas— $110-125 million.

The domestic political obstacles in attacking these restrictions are formidable. Yet it is precisely here that the biggest benefits can be achieved. The dismantling of such arrangements over the next generation is a reasonable objective of policy if we recognize our national interest in economic development overseas.

In economic development, as in other areas, we simply cannot have our cake and eat it too: we cannot expect our foreign aid to produce self-sustaining economic growth while we resist the domestic adjustments involved in accepting imports from the very countries we are helping.

Supplementing a policy of one-way free trade on products of particular importance to the less developed countries would be a policy of tariff preferences by way of advanced installments of tariff cuts in favor of less developed countries on products that are of major interest to other countries as well. At Punta del Este President Johnson announced a more flexible U.S. policy on this subject: "We are ready to explore with other industrialized countries— and with our people—the possibility of temporary preferential tariff advantages for all developing countries in the markets of all the industrialized countries."

One good way to implement this policy would be by granting advance installments of tariff cuts to the less developed countries. Congress should be asked to amend the Trade Expansion Act to permit the Kennedy Round tariff concessions to be granted immediately to the less developed countries rather than in stages over five years as the law presently requires. Concessions resulting, or expected to result, from future negotiating rounds should be made immediately available to the less developed countries in the same way. The great advantage of this approach is that it does not freeze the margin of preference and thus the rate of tariff protection against the developed countries.

President Johnson's statement envisages a system of preferences for *all* developing countries in the markets of *all* industrial countries. The United Kingdom and other countries have already expressed their support for this idea, but the Common Market countries, and particularly France, have favored *selective* preferences favoring some less developed countries (former African colonies) over others. The new policy announced by President Johnson offers an important opportunity to reverse the trend toward North-South preferential systems—a trend which threatens to fragment the world unduly into spheres of economic as well as political influence.

Of course, if the Common Market is not prepared to phase out its present selective preferences and grant preferences to all developing countries, the United States will face a difficult choice—whether or not to accept the special burdens attendant upon a preferential arrangement not accepted by a significant number of its industrialized trading partners.

II.   AID

This year marks the twentieth anniversary of General Marshall's famous speech at Harvard which launched the Marshall Plan. It is an appropriate time for the country which initiated the Marshall Plan and the countries which were its principal beneficiaries to launch a new Marshall Plan for the benefit of the less developed countries.

The United Nations and other bodies have recommended an aid effort by the developed countries equivalent to 1 percent of their gross national product. Despite rapid economic growth in the industrialized countries during the last few years, their foreign aid efforts have not expanded; thus, according to UN estimates, foreign aid as a proportion of GNP has slipped from 0.83 percent in 1961 to 0.69 percent in 1965. This trend can and must be reversed.

The heads of state of the Western industrialized countries should meet soon to chart a program of steady escalation of their foreign aid efforts. The objective should be achievement of the 1 percent target by 1975. This would mean a doubling of the total foreign aid effort of the United States and other countries, taking into account present rates of economic growth.

So far as possible this increased assistance should be made available through multilateral institutions or pursuant to multilateral arrangements such as the World Bank consortia. The United States recently agreed to finance 40 percent of the replenishment of the International Development Association, which makes loans of up to 50-year maturity at nominal rates of interest. The U.S. decision would make possible $600 million of additional IDA resources in fiscal '69, $800 million in fiscal '70 and $1 billion in fiscal '71—provided other industrialized countries are prepared to pay their share. Steady progress toward the 1 percent target would make possible further increases in IDA operations in the seventies and a substantial expansion in the activities of regional development banks operating in Africa, Latin America and Asia.

As Cold War tensions diminish, increasing efforts should be made to involve the Soviet Union and Eastern Europe in sharing the burden of economic aid. Development should be a cooperative, not a competitive enterprise. This objective may not be realizable immediately in all parts of the

70

world. But we can move toward it on a case-by-case basis. As a beginning, we might ask the Soviet Union to associate itself with the work of the World Bank consortium for India.

III. SELF-HELP BY THE LESS DEVELOPED COUNTRIES

Some of the greatest obstacles to dealing effectively with the trade and development problems of the less developed countries lie within these countries themselves. Many less developed countries are diverting to armaments scarce resources needed for economic development. Many have overvalued foreign exchange rates or severe inflation or inefficient state industries which make it impossible to export successfully, whatever trade policies are followed by the industrialized countries. Many are stifling their economic growth as well as their export capacity by excessive import restrictions which are driving up domestic production costs. Many of them are increasingly dependent on large imports of food because of failure to deal with the twin problems of food production and population growth.

The latter subject has received increasing recognition, but the ratio of talk to action is still distressingly high. Less than one family in one hundred in Latin America or the Indian subcontinent or Egypt or Indonesia has access to modern methods of family planning. Paradoxical as it may seem, the most effective way to deal with the "trade gap" and the 'aid gap" may be by closing the "family planning gap"—the gap between the number of families that have access to modern family planning techniques and the number that would make use of them if given the opportunity. As a result of this gap, approximately 40% of the children born in the world today are unwanted, in the sense that they would not have been born if their parents had been given the means to prevent it. Such a mass of children growing up without adequate education, housing, medical

71

care or family guidance, represents social dynamite as threatening to civilization in the long run as the hydrogen bomb.

It is significant that Dr. Raúl Prebisch, the Secretary-General of UNCTAD, has placed increasing emphasis on the internal responsibilities of the developing countries in his statements before UN meetings. He has called for "synchronized and convergent" policies of developed and less developed countries. Hopefully, his increasing concern with this subject will be reflected in the work of his agency. So far, however, this subject has been regarded as forbidden territory in UNCTAD. With one exception—regional trade arrangements among the developing countries—one looks in vain at the draft agenda for the second UNCTAD Conference for any significant reference to what these countries can and should do for themselves.

The United Nations has performed a great service in getting the developed countries to face up to their responsibilities to the less developed countries. But will it perform a similar service in getting the less developed countries to face up to their responsibilities to themselves?

IV. TECHNICAL AID AND ADVICE

The industrialized countries can play a vital role not only in encouraging the economic and social transformations necessary for development in the less developed countries but specifically in helping them to produce and sell effectively in world markets.

Through technical aid and advice, the industrialized countries can help the developing countries provide incentives (or end disincentives) to domestic or foreign business firms which are prepared to exploit export opportunities. Through such aid and advice, less developed countries can be helped to identify export possibilities, to produce more efficiently and to promote foreign sales through effective merchandising techniques.

The international agencies have been in the business of giving technical assistance and advice for many years. But they have not yet adequately focused their assistance on the trade promotion problem. What is now required is a major increase in technical assistance which can pay off in increased exports. The question is whether the many UN agencies which have a piece of this problem—UNCTAD, UNIDO, GATT, ILO, the UN Development Program and the World Bank—can work together effectively in coping with it.

Beyond technical assistance, we should encourage regular multilateral examination of the development policies and trade policies of less developed countries—policies which are now very poorly related to one another. Once again, we will have to find some reasonable division of labor and coordination for this purpose between the international agencies.

V. INTERNATIONAL MONETARY REFORM

The major increases in trade and aid needed to attack poverty on a world scale cannot be undertaken without fundamental reforms of the world's monetary system. For a decade now, the United States has been incurring substantial balance of payments deficits which have been financed through reductions in our gold stock and increases in foreign dollar holdings.

The U.S. payments deficit does not reflect any inability of our country to pay its way in world trade—on the contrary, we have consistently run large surpluses of exports over imports—but rather reflects the disproportionate burdens we are bearing in financing the growth and defense of the non-communist world. It may be some time before the problem can be cured by getting the European countries to pay a larger share for their own defense and to finance an increasing share of their new investment from their own capital markets.

A rational international monetary system would provide us this time. Unfortunately, our present system is based on gold, and the world stock of gold is growing much more slowly than the growth in world trade. Indeed, the world's monetary gold stock failed to grow at all during 1965 and 1966 due to diminished production and hoarding. To make matters worse, the German and French governments have converted substantial dollar balances into gold, thus reducing monetary reserves.

There are four main alternatives:

—Foreign governments can permit their dollar holdings to increase and abstain from cashing them in for gold. This they are apparently unwilling to do.

—The United States can try to cut down the deficit by curtailing aid and private investment abroad and tying aid to domestic procurement. This policy, which is already under way, has obvious disadvantages for ourselves, our European partners, and the less developed countries. The condition recently attached by the U.S. to its contribution to the replenishment of IDA is a case in point.

—The U.S. can begin to cut the link between the dollar and gold, either by refusing to sell gold to dollar holders or by declining to support the present gold price through gold purchases. These policies, advocated by some, would take us into uncharted and perhaps dangerous territory.

—We can adopt a plan for international monetary reform which would supplement the world's reserves and give us all additional time to deal on a multilateral basis with the problem of burden-sharing for defense and capital flow.

Present negotiations on international monetary reform have focused on two main alternatives—increasing the

74

drawing rights in the International Monetary Fund and creating new reserve assets ("paper gold"). As of this moment, the prospects for a substantial step forward in either of these directions are uncertain.

One of Dr. Prebisch's great contributions has been to help everyone to see more clearly the relationship between enlarging the world's stock of liquidity and doing more to help the less developed countries. If we are unable to do the first, we will not be able to do the second. Indeed, one of the lasting contributions of UNCTAD may be that it has forced the international community to deal with questions of trade, development and finance together—rather than in artificial compartments.

Although it may not be a political possibility for some time, the best approach would be to tackle the problems of development aid and monetary reform together, as a group of experts for UNCTAD has proposed. In other words, a new reserve unit could be created, and the national currencies paid in exchange for it by the developed countries could be used for long-term lending in the less developed world.

Is this a revolutionary program? Perhaps. But in revolutionary times revolutionary policies may be the only means of preserving traditional values.

Is it an unrealistic program? Perhaps. But those who say so have an obligation to state whether anything less than this can deal effectively with the problem of poverty in the world.

Is it an "unsound" program? Let us remember what Keynes once said: "A 'sound' man, alas, is a man who, when all his fellows are ruined, is ruined along with them."

CHAIRMAN CAREY: Thank you very much indeed, Professor Gardner.

Our next speaker, who is also the author of the outstanding summary of issues contained in the advance working paper, is a member of the New York Bar with many years of experience in both law and economics. After receiving the AB degree in 1936 and the LLB in 1938, both from Cornell, Professor Metzger spent twenty years as a Federal Attorney, fourteen of them in the Department of State.

He was Assistant Legal Advisor for Economic Affairs and advised Secretary of State Dulles in the negotiations leading to the Japanese Peace Treaty and during the Suez Canal dispute. He was instrumental in the preparation of the charter of the Inter-American Development Bank and in the establishment of the International Development Association. He was closely connected with the preparation of trade agreement legislation adopted by Congress in the late nineteen fifties, as well as being a consultant in the drafting of the Trade Agreement Act of 1962. He has advised the U.S. delegation in the drafting of a number of commodity agreements.

Since 1960 Mr. Metzger has taught as Professor of Law at Georgetown, and has also served as consultant to the State Department on trade policy, and as consultant to OECD, IAEA, and ICEM, as well as assisting private trade organizations and firms in international trade. He was the U.S. arbitrator in the 1964-1965 U.S.-Italian Aviation Arbitration. Professor Metzger is the author of three books and many articles.

Professor Metzger.

PROFESSOR STANLEY D. METZGER: Thank you very much, Mr. Carey. Being last man up after these distinguished predecessors, I feel very much like saying, "I have written a fairly extensive paper which I assume that you have all read, and there is very little else that I can add. Please ask any questions." But the chances of your having read it are not all that great and since the hour is not all that late, maybe I can just use some part of the thirty minutes in summarizing my position and indicating the areas of agreement and disagreement with the prior speakers.

Actually the areas of agreement are rather wide. The areas of disagreement relate, as they so often do, not to objectives but to ways and means of achieving them.

The two principal things that we are talking about, of course, are the enormous gaps in wealth between countries—and one that we have not mentioned so much but which is also extremely important—the enormous gaps of wealth within countries. This is particularly true in relation to the countries we are talking about, the so-called developing countries, the less developed countries, whatever term you wish to use.

I think there is common ground among us, probably amongst all in the room or at least among most, that these are two unhealthy things, these gaps—the width of the gaps, and that they should be closed. That is to say, the gaps between the developing countries and the developed countries in wealth and the gaps within countries. It is a little comforting to realize that there is no disagreement amongst us on these matters. Unfortunately, I don't think there is really that much agreement in the world at large on these basic propositions upon which we are in agreement.

Certainly the great difficulties that the less developed countries are having in creating what Dr. Prebisch so ably formulated as basic internal transformations, upon which I spent the first part of my paper, indicates that this is something which is obviously a matter of disagreement in most of the developing countries. The people who are running things there, who have the great majority of the wealth in these poor lands, are not very happy about closing the gap. Therein, of course, lies the major problem.

I think it is perfectly plain, Dr. Prebisch, and I couldn't agree with you more, that unless that is done, unless there is peaceful revolution, if you wish to put it that way, within the developing countries, everything else we are talking about is relatively meaningless. Trade measures and aid measures, or both combined, simply cannot accomplish the task. They must be supplemental to the basic internal transformations in the developing countries.

I wish that U Thant and the Pope had the kind of influence in these countries, inside, as they do among people like ourselves. Unfortunately, so far this has not proved to be the case. If UNCTAD under your leadership—which has been amazing in its results in a short time, and the world owes you a great debt—if UNCTAD could help the Pope and U Thant in this direction, this would be a major contribution, perhaps more than anything else that can be done in this area. But there is common ground amongst us even if this agreement doesn't percolate down where it might be more useful, namely, in the developing countries themselves.

There is also common ground amongst us with respect to closing the external gap—to assist, to supplement the internal transformation without which nothing is any good. There is also agreement amongst us that trade measures and aid measures are both necessary. I think there is no disagreement amongst us in respect of the kinds of aid measures and the magnitudes.

I perhaps am a little more ambitious than either Dr. Prebisch or Mr. Gardner. They are concerned about the developing countries securing one percent of the gross national product of each of the developed countries, a goal which was set in 1960, and which has not been reached yet by a very substantial margin. Dr. Prebisch would like to see that gap closed. Professor Gardner would like to see it closed and he puts a target of 1975 on it. I think it was an inadequate goal when it was set. I think it has become more inadequate now and I think that in terms of what needs to be done, there has got to be much more ambition. I noticed just a week or so ago, the executive secretary of the Economic Commission for Asia publicly stated at a session out in Tokyo, that the one percent goal—which has not been met—is quite inadequate in terms of ability to utilize more funds on the part of the less developed countries, in terms of price rises and in terms of related factors. So on this, there is common ground amongst us, except I think the one percent figure is an inadequate figure, if we are interested in seeing substantial growth at a relatively early date.

We are also agreed on trade measures, that is to say, that trade measures are essential. Here, however, is where we part company in a rather sharp way, namely, the type of trade measures. The major trade measure that is necessary in my judgment to assist the developing countries is a major assault upon protectionism in the developed countries, existing protectionism. This relates both to primary commodities and to manufactured articles. On the primary commodity side, the example that Dr. Prebisch gave, sugar growing—we are growing it in an economically inefficient manner. The production of other commodities such as cotton in developed countries which are more economically produced outside—this raw material protectionism, food stuffs protectionism in addition to sugar, this kind of protectionism affects hundreds of millions, if not billions, of dollars a year.

Unfortunately, there has not been a major assault upon this kind of protectionism. There has been almost an attitude of despair, so far as I have been able to see. The major proposals that have been put forward in the trade field by UNCTAD have not really touched this kind of protectionism.

The major proposals affecting trade in primary commodities put forward in UNCTAD have been two: one has been commodity agreements, and the second has been compensatory financing. Now, as to compensatory financing, as I point out in my paper, I agree fully that a system of compensatory financing which goes beyond that which has been agreed to by the Monetary Fund is advisable. I think the World Bank's proposal should be seriously debated and come into being in the shortest possible time. This is a proposal for a medium term, compensatory fi-

79

nancing scheme based upon a moving five year average and based upon the fact that anticipated export earnings are not measuring up to anticipations. To the extent that they don't measure up, financing should be had through a world bank instrumentality so that planning for financing development can proceed.

This kind of proposal does not interfere with the market, it does not attempt to set prices artificially at high levels. It accepts whatever fluctuations there are and provides money to the developing country so that it can be assured of a level of funds upon which to plan development. It is a supplementation of existing aid programs. It does not interfere with market forces and does not distort the trading system of the world.

This proposal, I think, is a perfectly sensible proposal and it is relevant to trade in primary commodities, but it is not relevant to decreasing protectionism in the primary commodity field on the part of developed countries. On the other hand, neither is the commodity agreement technique. This is the other area in which UNCTAD has been active.

In the primary commodity area, the only area in which commodity agreements can be made to work, as an UNCTAD paper recently said, is in the field of a handful of commodities where monopoly pricing is possible by developing countries—where there is no duplicated production in the developed country, and where there is no real danger of synthetics taking the place of the developing country's product. These are the products which the developing countries produce and which are not produced by the developed countries. In this area it is possible to have commodity agreements. The United States allows imports of coffee, tin, cocoa, tea and bananas, which are the five that qualify, duty free. We already allow these into this country without a penny's worth of duty. There is no protectionism on this area.

This is the area which qualifies for commodity agreements because this is where monopoly pricing can be

80

achieved to maximize the income of the developing country. But whatever the arguments for and against this technique may be, and I argue strongly against this technique of monopoly pricing, practically it doesn't do much for the underdeveloped countries. Coffee and tin you have agreements on. Bananas and tea are not likely candidates, and cocoa, upon which you are working—cocoa may or may not achieve a commodity agreement. When you have that, you have pretty much had it. There isn't much left.

In any event, whatever the arguments are—and I tried to outline as many devastating ones as I could throw off—this technique doesn't affect protectionism in the developing country at all, so that as for getting rid of the major factor which affects adversely trade in primary commodities with the developed countries, UNCTAD hasn't touched it. There has been no campaign mounted against protectionism in the primary commodity field on the part of the developed countries.

I would now go on to look at what the proposals have been for manufactured articles. The major proposals on manufactured articles that have been put forward by UNCTAD have been preferences on the one hand and regional arrangements on the the other.

To deal with the easiest one first, regional arrangements have practically nothing to do in the short run with trade between the developed countries and the developing countries. The purpose of regional arrangements is to have the developing countries trade more with each other. Only to the extent that this results in shifting of sources of supply in a major way does this affect trade between the developing countries and the developed countries.

In developing countries such as Latin America, ten percent of the total trade of the area is intra-Latin American. Since it is going to be 15 or 20 years before they create a common market as was stated at Punta del Este—if they ever get over very difficult problems— it is very clear that in short run terms the effect upon trade between the developing countries and the developed countries in the field of manufactured articles caused by regional arrangements is marginal. There are simply no real effects at present nor will there be for the foreseeable future.

Now let us look at the other end—to see what efforts have been made to get rid of protectionism in manufactured articles, having indicated earlier that there is no program for getting rid of protectionism in the primary comodity field. What about preferences? What are they designed to do? They are designed to get an advantage in a developed country market.

How many countries would be benefited by preferences as compared to how many would benefit by the elimination of protectionism in the developing countries? What is the major industrial product for which there would be a ready market? Cotton textiles I would suppose is the major product which developing countries are in a position to export with some success.

What would tariff preferences do in the cotton textile field? Well, the developed countries have already adopted the cotton textile long term agreement to which the developing countries agreed, which they didn't fight, so that if you had a tariff preference on cotton textiles, you wouldn't increase by one pound the amount of cotton textiles that would be exported from the developing countries. There might be a pick up on value because of the small difference in the tariff—but you wouldn't begin to secure the advantage from tariff preferences that you would have if you dismantled the quota system. The quota system has nothing whatever to do with preferences.

I would suspect that in fact if you ever did get preferences for the developing countries, that what you would run into immediately would be this neat trick of a tariff quota device which would be very nasty indeed. In the process you would have alienated yourselves from your liberal allies, your liberal trade allies in the developed countries who still take the position as I do, that MFN is good, and that a continued disintegration of MFN somehow does not give it new vitality, Dr. Prebisch. Destruction is destruction.

Moreover when you use a disguised form of aid you invite treating it as a deduction from straight aid. You will also invite loading it down with conditions which now accompany straight aid. You would invite restrictions on trade with Communist China, or with Cuba, or with the Soviet Union. You would invite 50-50 shipping laws. You would invite all the other conditions that countries impose when they give aid, because this is aid in the form of a trade measure. You would be asking for a destruction of MFN, and you would be asking for the kind of bilateral trade measures closely tied to aid that we saw evolving in a most ugly way in the prewar period.

I would summarize very briefly this way: The requirements of a more rapid economic development of the less developed countries consist of internal reforms of a character which signify basic transformations in their societies and drastic reduction of protectionism, and much larger amounts of straight economic aid by developed countries. In my judgment a number of the so-called trade solutions to lagging economic development, commodity agreements, preferences, regional arrangements, all the major ones that have been developed so far except compensatory financing, are marginal at best in their positive effects upon development, and carry serious side effects adverse to a world trading system.

I would like in passing to pick up this matter of President Johnson's supposed change of policy announced at Punta del Este on tariff preferences. As Professor Gardner indicated, this is a very carefully drafted statement, drafted well knowing that the Europeans are not beginning to agree to general preferences. They made it perfectly plain that they wanted selected preferences which they will negotiate out. We know perfectly well that the African countries are not going to give up their own special preferences. Last

83

year they asked the European countries to put special levies on tropical products from other less developed countries even though their own trade dropped with preferences— both agricultural and manufacturing.

This alleged change of policy by the U.S. was a little bit like the sleeves off the vest, if you examine it. The chances of general preferences happening in Europe, Dr. Prebisch, are not very great, just like the chances of Africans voluntarily accepting general preferences and giving up their special preferences, even though they are not worth much. To give up something that is not worth much for something that is worth less than not much is ridiculous.

My prescription—and what I would hope that you would do at UNCTAD—is to urge the developing countries to conserve the energies that they are now employing to secure trade solutions which are so meager in their effective resource transfer results and so capable of causing serious difficulties to the rational elements which persist in the existing trade system. They might then devote their energies, collectively, to securing greater amounts of foreign aid, directly and through compensatory financing and dismantling the protectionism by developing countries, and individually to internal transformation at home. If they were to shift the direction of their energies in this manner, they would be performing a signal service for themselves and mankind in general.

This is not to say that UNCTAD and their spokesmen and you particularly have not performed a service. I have said at the outset and I repeat: you performed a service for which we are all in your debt, because what you have done and what the countries which you represent have done is to focus the attention of the richer nations upon the deepening economic troubles of the poorer nations, and you have done this through an extremely diversified approach. The fact that you have not secured very much so far is not so important, because the important thing is that you stirred matters up dramatically, far beyond what orthodox methods might have succeeded in achieving.

It is now time, however, now that this interest has been stirred up, now that you have got a stage set—it is now time, it seems to me, to focus upon the important resource—begetting measures in order to secure substantial concrete benefits for the less developed countries. A greater sense of priorities is what I would urge.

Much greater direct aid in compensatory financing should be stressed and the small resources—transfer items such as commodity agreements and preferences should be dropped or postponed, and the drive toward regionalism should be transformed into a collective bargaining device to secure these other measures, the reduction of protectionism and collective bargaining for greater financial assistance.

It has become a cliche to say that the peoples of the underdeveloped world have awakened and we are going to be a witness to a rising crescendo of their demands for satisfaction and more just societies. Time is not on the side of greater order and prosperity. Time is on the side of greater chaos and more misery and if we—I mean both of us—are really serious in desiring to achieve economic development and minimize chaos and misery, we have to do a great deal more of the right things than presently appear on our agendas.

Thank you.

CHAIRMAN CAREY: Thank you very much, professor Metzger.

While questions from the audience are being collected, I would like to throw one at Professor Gardner. You have been critical of the proliferation of international organizations in this field, and have indicated that you think life should be more orderly in the community of nations in attacking these economic problems. I ask you, has there ever been a serious set of problems in history where the solution was approached with the kind of orderliness that you desire rather than with the disorder and proliferation of organizations that you seem to detect here?

In fact, Professor Gardner, is it not true that Dr. Prebisch's organization, UNCTAD, offered competition to the more established international organization set up by the General Agreement on Tariffs and Trade and by virtue of this competition gave it a real shot in the arm and advanced matters a great deal beyond where they would be today without Dr. Prebisch's organization?

PROFESSOR GARDNER: Of course it is a very good question and I would answer it this way, John: There has never been, as your question implies, a case of orderly adaptation to this kind of situation. Franklin Roosevelt used to say in the New Deal period that he would create four organizations to do a job because perhaps then one of them would actually do it.

I believe in shaking things up and I believe UNCTAD did shake things up. Things needed shaking up. The UN was not sufficiently effective in the economic field. The less developed countries had lost confidence in the Economic and Social Council and the General Assembly.

GATT had begun to move on the problems of the less developed countries in the 1961 meeting of the Contracting Parties and laid down the GATT Action Program in 1963, but there is no doubt that UNCTAD helped to stimulate GATT in this effort. The special GATT chapter on development approved in 1965 is an example.

UNCTAD also stimulated other international institutions, such as the International Bank and the International Monetary Fund. UNCTAD has pushed forward proposals on supplementary finance and preferences, and has underscored the interest of the less developed countries in the creation of adequate international liquidity. These are significant contributions.

But, things having been shaken up, I am concerned that things should also settle down. If we are going to achieve results there has to be the necessary coordination of effort. Valuable resources, and I have in mind people as well as dollars, are being consumed by the multiplication of secretariats and conferences. Many of these people might be better employed dealing with the problems of their countries at home.

I think Dr. Prebisch himself would agree that the time has come to consolidate UN efforts both in terms of numbers of conferences and secretariats.

CHAIRMAN CAREY: Here is a question from Mr. Nathaniel Winthrop, a member of the committee which organizes these forums. This is for Dr. Prebisch: would you, sir, care to comment on Mr. Gardner's point about the need for more self help by developing countries?

DR. PREBISCH: I fully agree with all that has been said here tonight about the need to combine, through a series of converging measures, the policies of developed countries with those of developing countries. I said before that the best international policy of economic cooperation is bound to fail if the developing countries do not take very important and far-reaching measures of their own.

At the same time, internal reforms, structural changes in developing countries, would not have a great impact on their rate of growth, if they are not accompanied by a vigorous policy of international cooperation. So that I think that the real problem that has to be solved is how to combine external and internal measures; external measures that should be taken by developed countries with internal measures to be taken by the developing countries.

Here again I see a great merit in the results of the Punta del Este meeting, which is clear proof that in certain fields related to trade and development there is the possibility of combining measures. Latin American countries have decided to create a common market of their own. The United States has promised support to this effort and also to ex-

87

plore trade policy measures to help the export of manufactured goods from developing to developed countries.

This is a good example of combination of measures and it should be extended to the whole field of trade and development.

CHAIRMAN CAREY: Here is a question which I would like to ask Professor Metzger to respond to, if he cares to. Considering the drain of U.S. resources due to Vietnam and to the intensification of an adverse balance of payments, and considering the growing protectionism of the Common Market evident in the Kennedy Round negotiations, how realistic is it to propose increased aid, less protectionism by the U.S., and new monetary liquidity? Given the difficulty of moving in these areas, isn't the only other meaningful alternative to adopt price raising commodity agreements, tariff preferences and supplementary financing as proposed by UNCTAD until the less developed countries reach take-off point—that is, for a limited period of time?

PROFESSOR METZGER: I agree it is tough all over. But I still would rather be in the frying pan than in the fire. Sure it is difficult and as long as there is an imbalance of payments, it is going to be harder to get more foreign aid. As long as we are in the Vietnam situation we will likely continue to be in imbalance of payments difficulties. I say, let us close out the Vietnam war as soon as possible. This is one thing that would help.

In connection with this, I would suggest to Dr. Prebisch that maybe he and UNCTAD could lend their voice to the Pope's and U Thant's in seeking to impress upon all participants in the Vietnam war, not bearing down on one, but all the interests—the interests of 77 countries, in having them all cease and desist from this affair so that the resulting savings could be utilized for economic development of less developed countries. I think to the extent that the voice of the 77 was heard throughout the land, all lands—

in Hanoi, Peking, Moscow, Saigon, Washington, to the extent that it was heard, perhaps you have more battalions than the Pope or U Thant has in that sense, and perhaps it might help matters.

There is no easy answer. The job of even keeping up past levels of appropriations for foreign aid is extremely difficult, as we are finding in Washington now. To talk about increasing them has an air of immediate unreality, but I should add not nearly as unreal as these other measures are at best in terms of being resource-beginning measures—they simply don't measure up. They are tickling the problem at the edges rather than hitting for the jugular.

CHAIRMAN CAREY: The next question is for Professor Gardner. Why is direct private foreign investment not among the five points proposed as gap closers? Is a U.S. tax incentive for foreign investment feasible?

PROFESSOR GARDNER: I suppose the only honest answer to that question is, I couldn't fit more than five points into thirty minutes. Yes, in these halls, it would be inappropriate not to come out with a resounding call for private investment and I am very strong for this. This goes almost without saying.

I think the package of tax incentives which the Kennedy Administration sent to Congress in 1963 ought to be dusted off and looked at again. Here again the balance of payments comes into the picture. Those tax proposals were withdrawn partly because it was felt that such drastic measures to promote capital outflow would have no chance of acceptance in view of the payments deficit.

This is why I come back again to the necessary link between trade, aid and monetary reform. I don't see how we can solve any one of these problems unless we solve the other two. We should recapture the spirit of the wartime and early post-war period when these three problems were looked at together. I think in recent years we have sometimes failed because we fragmented them artificially. Dr.

89

Prebisch and UNCTAD have performed a great service in forcing us to look at all three problems together.

CHAIRMAN CAREY: Dr. Prebisch, may I put a question to you, sir, from Dr. Martin Domke, another member of the committee which presents these Hammarskjöld Forums. One of our internal measures which worked well in Europe was the prevention of capital flight. Why has this not been employed in Latin America?

DR. PREBISCH: I wish that we could discover a proper way of preventing capital flight. It is highly desirable, but first it is desirable to stop inflation.

Perhaps the most important factor causing capital flight is inflation. I don't think that it is wrong to take direct control measures but this is very difficult. And I am talking as a former banker who recalls the experience of Hitler's Germany when, even under that drastic dictatorial period, it was impossible to control capital flight. This is why I insist —and have insisted for years—on the need to combine vigorous development policies with vigorous monetary policies, a noninflationary monetary policy to promote good development.

CHAIRMAN CAREY: Here is a question for Professor Metzger. To reduce the external trade gap and to enhance possibilities for the development of internal markets, what kinds of incentives do you see as effective for increased foreign private investment to increase exports from developing countries and to provide increased internal transformation, especially in the area of joint ventures, private and private-government arrangements?

PROFESSOR METZGER: I am not quite clear that I have it all. So far as incentives are concerned, I think the U.S. program of investment guarantees is quite good. The all-risk policy might be considered quite seriously, where it is related to diversification of production in the developing country.

I think here you have a form of direct foreign assistance of a contingent variety. It is like the old guarantee of private loans which, when the IBRD was created back in 1944, most people thought it would be its principal function. In fact, it has not been used at all because direct loans have been the method. But I see no reason not to use the all-risk guaranty to supplement direct aid where it is tied to development or to diversification in industry in the developing country.

I think that every effort to supplement direct government lending through guarantees of private investment which can add a great deal in new industry formation, diversification and the like, should be encouraged. It is not as much of a drain as a direct aid transfer, because it is contingent—a guarantee. If one is quite careful, one could soon have less than one hundred cents on the dollar as a guarantee. One could soon reduce it to fifty and then forty, and thirty percent, and twenty percent, a safe figure, so that one could make the dollar go a little bit further. I think it is worth exploring. I see that there have been some tentative moves in this direction very recently, but more could be done.

CHAIRMAN CAREY: Dr. Prebisch, here is a question which I would like to ask you, sir. I would like to supplement it with one of my own: Why was UNIDO established? What is its purpose as distinct from other UN organizations? I myself would like to ask, what is the relationship between your organization, UNCTAD, and UNCITRAL, the new UN Commission on International Trade Law? Could you clarify for us, sir, the relationship among these various strangely named creatures?

DR. PREBISCH: That reminds me of my arrival in Chile when I joined the United Nations Economic Commission for Latin America some twenty years ago. I was then instructed about some forty international institutions. Of course there are many more now. The same night I was invited to the house of a new friend, and those present started to talk about "Senta." I said, "what institution is that?" He said, "no, that's the lady of the house!"

The relationship of UNCITRAL with UNCTAD is the following: there are a number of problems in international trade law where it is necessary to combine the knowledge and experience of economists and the knowledge and experience of legal minds so that the General Assembly, in creating this Commission, decided to establish such a link between the two.

The same happened in relation to UNIDO, the Organization for Industrial Development. There was from the inception of the United Nations a Food and Agricultural Organization, FAO, but not an industrial organization. The objective of UNIDO is to work in the industrial field, and, from the beginning, we have tried to cooperate very closely with it in some specific problems. For instance, we arrived at the decision to combine the efforts of the regional commissions of the United Nations, the forces of UNIDO, and UNCTAD, in order to promote a joint export program for developing countries with the full support of the UN Development Program. This is the only way to avoid the enormous risk of proliferation to which Dr. Gardner has made reference. To work together, not to "coordinate", but to really work together, to join resources of different organizations to achieve common objectives.

CHAIRMAN CAREY: The final question, and this is a rather stimulating one, I think I will put to Professor Metzger. Why not establish, boldly, imaginatively, and as soon as possible, a common, single, world-wide currency?

PROFESSOR METZGER: Well, from my point of view it would be fine, if there were one language, English, and one currency, the dollar. The reason, of course, that it is not possible to do it boldly, imaginatively or weakly or foolishly, is that a currency system is a reflection of the economic solidity which it serves. It tends to reflect the weaknesses, perhaps more than the strength, and the reason is that one currency reflecting the strengths and weaknesses of the world today, unless it were backed by the reserve of one country which was recognized to be strong, and was traded in, unless it was the dollar, would simply not keep a value from day to day, which anybody could depend on.

The real difficulty in a common currency, as the Europeans are finding out, is that it is a reflection of unity, economic unity. I would hope some day we could have one world, but I am afraid it is a little bit far off.

CHAIRMAN CAREY: Finally, I would like to ask our other speakers, beginning with Dr. Prebisch, if they would like to take three minutes for summation?

DR. PREBISCH: Thank you, Mr. Carey. Very willingly, sir. I would like to comment on the excellent presentation of Professor Metzger, after congratulating my friend Dick Gardner, for his magnificent work.

Professor Metzger, you said UNCTAD has not paid attention to the question of access to markets. This is not so. Access to markets is something about which, at every meeting of the Commodity Committee, as well as in the UNCTAD Conference three years ago, there has been continuous insistence, particularly with a new emphasis on lessening the various barriers that are impeding the access of primary products of great interest to the developing of countries into the markets of the industrial centers.

The other subject that I would like to mention is this: you do not seem to attach importance to regional integration or intraregional trade due to the fact that it is a complex task, the results of which may not be felt in the immediate future. Are you in favor of birth control?

PROFESSOR METZGER: Yes.

DR. PREBISCH: In twenty years time?

PROFESSOR METZGER: That is not part of my program.

93

DR. PREBISCH: Birth control will take time. Its effects on the labor force may not be felt before some 20 years. Yet, in the next twenty years those already having been born will have to be absorbed somehow by the various sectors of the economy of the developing nations, particularly the modern sector, that is to say, industry primarily. We cannot wait 20 years.

But a common market can produce effects much before—in three or four years, if there is really a bold policy of elimination and reduction of trade restrictions among the participating countries; the effects would be considerable.

In the case of Latin America, for example, take into consideration that in the iron and steel industry the present annual production is around six million tons. In ten years more, Latin America should be able to produce some fifteen million tons of iron and steel in order to meet the growing demand and the only way to produce this economically is through the gradual formation of a more integrated regional iron and steel industry which could also help to lower the corresponding internal tariffs.

Let us not forget that foresight is essential in economic policy. We have to escalate a series of measures, some measures that will have immediate effects, some other measures that will have effects in three or four years, and some that will have effects in ten or twenty years.

Another argument that you presented is that industrial and trade relations between the Latin American countries are presently so weak, so unimportant that they do not seem to give great support to the common market. This is true. But, precisely, in order to promote the further development of industry and trade in the developing world, among Latin American countries in the case in point, it is indispensable to create a common market. If we do not create the common market in Latin America, trade among Latin American countries will continue to be at a very low level.

Finally, in relation to preferences, time is very short to take up one by one all of your arguments, Professor Metzger, but let me deal with one of them at least. You are dubious about the possibility of getting some kind of agreement with the European Common Market about preferences. It is true that the French attitude has been, as you have indicated, in favor of a selective system by goods and by countries, but that is very bad in my view and in this I fully agree with you. But it is nonetheless true that not all the Six think the same way. The Germans, for instance, have expressed themselves in favor of a general system of non-discriminatory preferences applied to all developing countries. So that there is a chance of being able to persuade the European Common Market, if the United States makes an effort in this sense, accompanied by the "77"—I think that it is worthwhile to take advantage of this coincidence of views to work toward what I consider a very wise policy.

PROFESSOR GARDNER: I find myself in a strange position: I agree with both of my colleagues. It was a wise man that once said that "both and" is the road to hell and "either or" is the road to heaven. But in this case I am a "both and" man.

I agree with Professor Metzger that UNCTAD ought to emphasize aid and self help rather more than it has done hitherto and that UNCTAD should not over-estimate the resource transfers that are attendant upon changes in the trade mechanism. I share the skepticism which he has expressed in his truly magnificent paper.

I share the skepticism he expresses on commodity agreements. I also agree with him that the preference issue has been exaggerated. I don't think the benefits will be as great as some suppose.

On the other hand, I agree with Dr. Prebisch on a number of things. I was surprised to have Professor Metzger suggest that Dr. Prebisch and I were being too cautious.

95

If my proposal on aid were accepted—steady escalation of effort to meet the one percent target in 1975—it would mean more than a doubling of existing aid. In 1975, for example, the U.S. will have a one trillion dollar GNP; one percent of that would be ten billion dollars.

We all outdo one another in setting higher aid targets, but I think we all have to admit there is some limit to the absorptive capacity of less developed countries and to the administrative capacity of governmental agencies. If we can get to that one per cent target in 1975, that would be quite an achievement.

On preferences: I share Professor Metzger's commitment to the most-favored-nation principle, but I would suggest that we are not dealing with an ideal world.

If we were already in a world of free multilateral trade it would be one thing, but we are in a world where there are already vertical preferential arrangements. That is a very unhealthy type of world and has all the implications of spheres of influence.

I think global preferences provide a useful way of getting rid of this north-south preferential system and therefore we should accept them on that basis.

On regional arrangements: once again, if we were in a free multilateral world, regional preferences and customs unions would not look so good. But we are in a world of highly protectionist, small national markets. If we can move from that to regional trade, I think we are moving in a very useful direction.

On birth control: Dr. Prebisch suggested it would take twenty years for a birth control policy to pay off. I must respectfully disagree. Birth control surely pays off right away. Having fewer children means that now there should be less of a drain on the national economy for food, education, housing and basic services.

DR. PREBISCH: I was referring to the labor force.

PROFESSOR GARDNER: Finally, on fragmentation of effort: I am not sure that sending out committees is really enough. We are moving in the UN to a desperate situation where everyone is trying to coordinate everybody else. A committee cannot always coordinate the institutions from which the representatives on the committee have been chosen.

I think the UN will have to come soon to a fundamental consolidation and reorganization, with a new Director-General for Economic Affairs, ranking second only to the Secretary-General himself, and armed with authority to bring this whole thing under control.

CHAIRMAN CAREY: Ladies and gentlemen, we have all been indeed privileged to hear from two of our outstanding lawyer-economists in the United States, and one of the outstanding economists of the whole world tonight, dealing with what the Secretary-General of the United Nations has called the most crucial and the most challenging long term struggle of this century.

Thank you and good night.

Bibliography on Law and
Policy Making for Trade Among
"Have" and "Have-Not" Nations

Prepared by ANTHONY P. GRECH

*Librarian, The Association of the
Bar of the City of New York*

GENERAL

Balassa, Bela A. Trade prospects for developing countries. Homewood, Ill., Erwin. 1964. 450p.

Brendel, Gerhard. The developing countries and world trade. 1965. 4 German For. Policy 443-51.

Burenstan, Linder S. Trade and trade policy for development. New York, Praeger, 1967. 179p.

Butler, W. Trade and the less devcloped areas. 1963. 41 For. Aff. 372-83.

Chandavarkar, A. G. Trade relations between developed and developing economies in the context of economic development. April 1964. 5 Int'l Studies (Bombay) 377-400.

Conference on International Trade and Investment, 2nd, Yale Law School, 1962. International financing and investment; proceedings, edited by John F. McDaniels ... With an introd. by James G. Johnson, Jr. Dobbs Ferry, N. Y., Published for the World Community Association by Oceana. 1964. 738p.

Cooper, C. A. and Massell, B. F. Toward a general theory of customs unions for developing countries. Santa Monica, Calif. 1965. 27p. (Rand Corp. paper P-2919-1)

Davis, Frederick. The regulation and control of foreign trade. 1966. 66 Colum. L. Rev. 1428-60.

De Vries, Margaret G. Trade and exchange policy and economic development: two decades of evolving views. March 1966. 18 Oxford Econ. Pap. 19-44.

Ebb, Lawrence F. Regulation and protection of international business. St. Paul, West. 1964. (Part III, National and international regulation of government barriers to international trade, pp.679-876)

The encouragement and protection of investment in developing countries; a report of a conference held on 28 & 29 Sept. 1961 under joint auspices of Federal Trust for Education and Research, The British Institute of International and Comparative

Law, the Institute of Advanced Legal Studies. London. 1962. 85p. (Int'l. & Comp. L. Q. Supp. Pub. no. 3)

Evans, John. U.S. trade policy. New York, Published for the Council on Foreign Relations by Harper. 1967. 105p.

Fatouros, A. A. Comments on international law and economic development. 1966. 60 Am. Soc'y Int'l L. 18-28.

Feliciano, Florentino P. Comments on "The relevance of international law to the development process." 1966. 60 Am. Soc'y Int'l L. Proc. 15-17.

Frank, Isaiah. New perspectives on trade and development. 1967. 45 For. Aff. 520-40.

Friedman, Irving S. In defence of development. 1965. 22 World Today 142-51.

Friedmann, Wolfgang G. The relevance of international law to the processes of economic and social development. 1966. 60 Am. Soc'y Int'l L. Proc. 8-15.

Friedmann, Wolfgang G., Kalmanoff, George and Meagher, Robert F. International financial aid. New York, Columbia Univ. Press. 1966. 498p.

Galbraith, V. L. World trade in transition. Washington, Public Affairs Press. 1965. 104p.

Gardiner, R. K. A. Development and trade in Africa. 1966. 65 African Aff. 1-14.

Gardner, Richard N.
  In pursuit of world order; U.S. foreign policy and international organizations. Rev. ed. New York, Praeger, 1966. 278p.
  Legal-economic problems of international trade. 1961. 61 Colum. L. Rev. 313-21.
  New directions in U.S. foreign policy. New York, Foreign Policy Assn. 1959. 77p. (Headline series no. 133)
  Organizing world trade-a challenge for American lawyers. 1957. 12 Record 202-26.
  Sterling-dollar diplomacy. Rev. ed. New York, McGraw-Hill. 1967.
  World trade in crisis: legal and policy issues (in Bar Association of St. Louis. The rule of law at the international level. St. Louis, 1965, pp.12-25)

Hoffman, Paul G. *Rx* for a split-level world. Summer 1966. 1 Colum. J. World Bus. 43-49.

Howell, David. New paths for world trade. 1965. 3 J. Common Market Studies 293-301.

International Association of Legal Science. Les aspects juridiques du dévelopement économique. Legal aspects of economic development. Études...sous la direction de André Tunc. Paris, Dalloz. 1966. 206p.

Johnson, Harry G. Economic policies toward less developed countries. Washington, Brookings Institution. 1967. 279pp.

Johnson, Harry G. and Kenen, Peter B. Trade and development: two lectures presented at the Graduate institute of international studies in Geneva. Genève, Librairie Droz. 1965. 49p.

Joyce, James Avery. Decade of development; the challenge of the underdeveloped nations. New York, Coward-McCann. 1967. 121p. (Challenge books)

Kaldor, Nicholas. International trade and economic development. 1964. 2 J. Modern African Studies 491-509.

Kitamura, Hiroshi. Foreign trade problems in planned economic development (in Berrill, Kenneth, ed. Economic development with special reference to East Asia; proceedings of a conference held by the International economic association. London, Macmillan, 1964, pp.191-211)

Krivine, David, ed. Fiscal and monetary problems in developing states. New York, Praeger. 1967. 400p.

Lacharrière, Guy de. Commerce extérieur et sous-développement. Paris, Presses Universitaires de France. 1964. 279p .

Lakdawala, D. T. Commercial policy and economic growth (in Das Gupta, A. K., ed. Trade theory and commercial policy in relation to underdeveloped countries; proceedings of the Seminar on international trade held under the auspices of the Indian School of International Studies in March 1963. London, Asia Pub. House, 1965, pp. 29-41)

Lasswell, Harold D. The relevance of international law to the development process. 1966. 60 Am. Soc'y Int'l L. Proc. 1-8.

Lewis, W. Arthur. Economic development and world trade (in Robinson, E. A. G., ed. Problems in economic development; proceedings of a conference held by the Economic association. London, Macmillan, 1965, pp. 483-97)

Little, Ian Malcolm David. International aid; a discussion of the flow of public resources from rich to poor countries, by Little and J. M. Clifford. Chicago, Aldine Pub. 1966. 302p.

MacBean, Alasdair I. Causes of excessive fluctuation in export proceeds of underdeveloped countries. Nov. 1964. 26 Bull. Oxford Univ. Inst. Econ. Statist. 323-41.

Marcus, E. and Marcus, M. R. International trade and finance. New York, Pitman. 1965. 616p.

Meier, Gerald. International trade and development. New York, Harper & Row. 1963. 208p.

Metzger, Stanley D.
Development of rules relating to international trade. 1959. 59 Am. Soc'y Int'l L. Proc. 28-33.

International law, trade and finance; realities and prospects. Dobbs Ferry, N. Y., Oceana. 1962. 184p.

Law of international trade: documents and readings. Washington, Lerner. 1966. 2v.

101

United States foreign trade: past, present and future. 1961. 6 Vill. L. Rev. 503-13.

National Council of Applied Economic Research. Development without aid. New Delhi. 1966. 95p. (Its Occasional paper, 15)

Nwogugu, E. I. The legal problems of foreign investment in developing countries. Dobbs Ferry, N. Y., Oceana. 1965. 320p.

Onitiri, H. M. A. The terms of trade (in Robinson, E. A. G., ed. Problems in economic development; proceedings of a conference held by the International economic association. London, Macmillan, 1965, pp.510-29)

Parthasarthy, G. The rich and the poor nations and international economic co-operation. 1963. 12 Indian Yb. Int'l Aff. 465-86.

Patterson, Gardner. Discrimination in international trade: the policy issues, 1945-1965. Princeton, Princeton Univ. Press. 1966. 414p.

Paul, A. The role of trade in a development program (in Conference on middle East affairs, 17th Washington, 1963. Developmental revolution. Washington, 1963, pp.226-36)

Pincus, John A. Trade, aid and development; the rich and poor nations. New York, Published for the Council on Foreign Relations by McGraw-Hill. 1967. 400p.

Prebisch, Raúl. Informe . . . sobre comercio y desarrollo. 1964. Rev. de Economía Política 205-354.

Prebisch, Raúl. Some fundamental problems of world trade. 1966. 3 (2) U.N. Monthly Chronicle 44-52.

Pryor, Frederic L. Economic growth and the terms of trade. March 1966. 18 Oxford Econ. Pap. 45-57.

Robinson, Austin. Foreign trade in a developing economy (in Berrill, Kenneth, ed. Economic development with special reference to East Asia; proceedings of a conference held by the International economic association. London, Macmillan, 1964, pp.212-27)

Sarre, David A. Godwin. The law of international trade and the developing countries. 1963. J. Bus. L. 108-18.

Seers, Dudley. International trade and development . . . the special interests of Africa (in Stewart, I. G. & Ord, H. W., eds. African primary products and international trade; papers delivered at an international seminar in the Univ. of Edinburgh. Sept. 1964. Edinburgh Univ. Press, 1965, pp. 19-25)

Seidman, R. M. Law and economic development in independent English-speaking subSaharan Africa. 1966. Wis. L. Rev. 999-1070.

Seminar on International Trade, Delhi, 1963. Trade theory and commercial policy in relation to underdeveloped countries; proceedings, edited by A. K. Das Gupta. New York, Asia Pub. House, 1965. 108p.

102

Society for International Development. International development, 1965 edition by Stefan H. Rabock and Leo M. Solomon. Dobbs Ferry, N. Y., Oceana. 1966. 197p.

Stanovnik, J. Aid, trade and economic development: the changing political context. 1964. 42 For. Aff. 242-54.

Stern, R. M. Policies for trade and development. May 1964. 548 Int'l Conciliation 1-63.

Stewart, Charles F. and Simmons, George B., comps. A bibliography of international business. New York, Columbia Univ. Press. 1964. 603p.

Surrey, Walter S. and Shaw, Crawford, eds. A lawyer's guide to international business transactions. Philadelphia, Joint Committee on Continuing Legal Education. 1963. 1071p.

Thompson, Dennis, ed. Expansion of world trade, legal problems and techniques, a conference report published under the auspices of the British Institute of International and Comparative Law. London, Stevens. 1965. 81p.

Trade problems between countries having different economic and social systems. Nov. 1964. 16 Econ. Bull. Europe 31-87.

United Nations. Department of Economic and Social Affairs. World economic survey, 1963. Pt. 1: Trade and development; trends, needs and policies. New York. 1964. 306p. (ST/ECA/84; E/3908)

U.S. Library of Congress. Legislative Reference Service. Free trade, tariff legislation, and common markets for the western hemisphere. Washington, Gov't Print. Off. 1962. 70p.

U.S. Tariff Commission. List of selected publications relating to United States tariff and commercial policy and to the general agreement on tariffs and trade. 7th ed. March. 1963. 18p. (TC pubn. 83)

Vartikar, V. S. The role of commercial policy in the development of a subsistence economy. 1965. 95 Weltwirtsch Archiv. 102-25.

Woods, George D. The development decade in the balance. 1966. 44 For. Aff. 206-15.

TRADE EXPANSION ACT OF 1962
AND THE KENNEDY ROUND

Association of the Bar of the City of New York. Comm. on Federal Legislation. The proposed trade expansion act of 1962. 1962. 17 Record 331-34.

Ball, George W.
  Major aspects of the trade expansion act. 1962. 46 Dep't State Bull. 597-605.
  The meaning of the trade expansion act. 1962. A. B. A. Sec. Int'l & Comp. L. 50-55.

Blau, Clarence I. Trade expansion act of 1962. 1962. 4 Inst. on Private Invest. Abroad 185-93.

Blumenthal, M. The Kennedy round. 1965. 52 Dep't State Bull. 628-35.

Brainard, Harry G.
 The trade expansion act—1962. Winter 1963. 11 Bus. Topics 7-19.
 The trade expansion act—1962 (in Michigan State University, East Lansing. Institute for international business management studies. International dimensions in business. East Lansing, 1966, pp. 63-75)

Bush, P. and Curtis, T. A minority challenge to the trade act (in Steel, R. U.S. foreign trade policy. N.Y., Wilson, 1962, pp. 45-54)

Camps, M. The Kennedy round. 1964. 20 World Today 215-22.

Chayes, Abram. The proposed trade expansion act of 1962. 1962. 17 Record 335-45.

Clubb, Bruce E.
 Dismantling trade barriers: implementation of the trade expansion act. 1965. U. Ill. L. F. 366-98.
 Dismantling trade barriers: implementation of the trade expansion act (in La Fave, Wayne R. & Hay, Peter, eds. International trade, investment and organization. Urbana, Univ. of Ill. Press, 1967, pp.32-64)

Congressional Quarterly. Trade expansion act of 1962. Washington, Congressional Quarterly. 1962. 61p.

Coppock, J. D. Trade policy choices facing the United States. 1962. 46 Dep't State Bull. 1027-31.

Dale, William B. U.S. programs to expand international trade. 1962. 6 Pat., T. M. & Cr. J. of Res. & Ed. (Confer. no.) 132-38.

Dugimont, J. Les négociations du Kennedy round. Avril 1966. Etudes Economiques 85-104.

Givens, Richard A. The search for an alternative to protection. 1961. 30 Fordham L. Rev. 17-58.

Gossett, W. T. The Kennedy round: progress and promise. 1963. 49 Dep't State Bull. 291-96.

Greggersen, J. Trade agreements program and trade expansion act of 1962. Der vereingten staaten von Amerika. Köln. 1964. 1v.

Herter, Christian A.
 The Kennedy round: a progress report. 1965. 53 Dep't State Bull. 31-34.
 U.S. aims in the Kennedy round. 1964. 2 Atl. Community Q. 240-46.

Jacobi, Klaus. Die Kennedy-runde des GATT und die schweiz. Sonderabdruck aus "Schweizer monatshefte" 44. Jahr, Heft. 4. Juli 1964, 28p.

Kenen, Peter B. The trade expansion act of 1962 and U.S. tariff policy. 1962. 2 Am. Rev. 118-47.

Kennedy, John F. A new foreign trade program. 1962. 46 Dep't State Bull. 231-38.

La loi Américaine "d'expansion du commerce," réflexions sur quelques problèmes futurs. 1963. 55 Rev. du Marché Commun 67-71.

La "longue marche" du Kennedy round. 1964. 74 Rev. du Marché Commun 480-85.

Mathews, C. Non-tariff import barriers and the Kennedy round. 1965. 2 Common Market L. Rev. 403-19.

Metzger, Stanley D.
The prospects for the Kennedy round. 1965. J. Bus. L. 103-13.
Trade agreements and the Kennedy round. Fairfax, Va., Coiner Pub. 1964. 119p.
The trade expansion act of 1962. 1963. 51 Geo. L. J. 425-69.

La négociation Kennedy, quelques points d'interrogation. 1966. 93 Rev. du Marché Commun 633-37.

Obstacles to the trade of less-developed countries (in Contracting parties to the General agreement on tariffs and trade. Proceedings of the meeting of ministers. Nov. 27-30, 1961, Geneva, 1962, pp.89-170)

Reischer, Otto Richard. Trade adjustment in theory and practice. Prepared for the subcom. on Foreign economic policy of the Joint economic committee. Congress of the United States. Washington, Gov't Print. Off. 1961. 98p.

Robertson, J. Adjustment assistance under the trade expansion act of 1962: a will-o-the-wisp. 1965. 33 Geo. Wash. L. Rev. 1088-1125.

Roussakis, Emmanuel N. Les négociations Kennedy et la politique commerciale des Etats-Unis d'Amérique. 1964. 68 Rev. du Marché Commun 168-73.

Sonderegger, Fritz. Die Kennedy-runde als integrations-instrument. May 25, 1966. 21 Europa-Archiv 377-82.

Steel, R. U.S. foreign trade policy. New York, Wilson. 1962. 200p.

Surrey, Walter S. Legal problems to be encountered in the operation of the trade expansion act of 1962. 1963. 41 N.C.L. Rev. 389-400.

Trade expansion act of 1962. 1962. 1 Int'l Leg. Materials 340-71.

Triffin, R. The trade expansion act of 1962. 1962. 56 Am. Soc'y Int'l L. Proc. 139-57.

U.S. Congress. House. Comm. on Ways and Means.
(87.2) Trade expansion act of 1962. Hearings . . . on H. R. 9900, a bill to promote the general welfare, foreign policy, and security of the United States through international trade agreements. Washington, Gov't Print. Off. 1962. 6pts.
(87.2) Trade expansion act of 1962. Report to accompany H. R. 11970, a bill to promote the general welfare, foreign policy, and security of the United States through international trade agreements and through adjustment assistance to domestic agriculture and labor and for other purposes. Washington, Gov't Print. Off. 1962. 104p.

U.S. Congress. Senate. Comm. on Finance. (87.2) Trade expansion act of 1962. Hearings ... on H. R. 11970, an act to promote the general welfare, foreign policy and security of the United States through international trade agreements. Washington, Gov't Print. Off. 1962. 5pts.

U.S. Congress. House. Comm. on Ways and Means. Brief digest of direct statements of public witnesses presented in personal appearances ... at hearings on H. R. 9900, trade expansion act of 1962, together with summary of principal recommendations as to amendment of the bill. Washington, Gov't Pint. Off. 1962. 33p.

Weiss, Leonard W. The new trade expansion act. Washington, U.S. Department of State. 1962. 18p. (Dep't State pub. 7372)

Wells, S. J. The Kennedy round. 1966. 20 Yb. World Aff. 201-19.

Wilbur, Richard C. International aspects of United States trade policy. 1961. 37 Notre Dame Law. 98-105.

Wortmann, Herman R. Is the Kennedy round a giant step toward trade liberalization? Spring 1965. 8 Bus. Horizons 25-34.

U.N. CONFERENCE ON TRADE AND DEVELOPMENT

Ali, S. A. United Nations conference on trade and development. 1964. 17 Pakistan Horizon 262-71.

Balogh, T. Notes on the United Nations conference on trade and development. Feb. 1964. 26 Bull. Oxford U. Inst. of Econ. & Statist. 21-37.

Bloch, Henry Simon. The challenge of the world trade conference. New York, Columbia Univ. Press. 1965. 56p.

Bochet, B. Notes sur l'organisation et les travaux de la conférence des Nations Unies sur le commerce et le développement. Oct/ Dec. 1964. 5 Tiers-Monde 865-84.

La conférence de l'ONU sur le commerce et le développement. Sept. 1964. 19 Développement et Civilisations 20-63.

Dell, Sidney. UNCTAD: retrospect and prospect (in Swift, Richard N., ed. Annual review of United Nations affairs, 1964-1965. Dobbs Ferry, N. Y., Oceana, 1966, pp. 52-85)

Dharma, Kumar. U.N. conference on trade and development. Sept. 1965. 21 India Q. 311-15.

Etra, Aaron. Time for a change: the U.N. conference on trade and development. 1966. 1 Rev. Belge de Droit Int'l 50-67.

Fletcher, Arthur. What UNCTAD is about. 1964. 43 Far East. Econ. Rev. 669-70.

Forthomme, P. A. Some implications of the U.N. conference on trade and development. Jan. 1965. 20 Belgian Trade Rev. 12-17.

Frank, I. Aid, trade and economic development: issues before the U.N. conference. 1964. 42 For. Aff. 210-26.

Gal-Edd, I. A framework for trade between developed and less-developed countries (in U.N. conference on trade and development. Geneva, 1964. Proceedings, vol. 5, pp. 493-501)

Gall, H. Conferencia de las Naciones Unidas sobre comercio y desarrollo. 1964. 5 Foro Internacional (Mexico) 99-129.

Gardner, Richard N. GATT and the United Nations conference on trade and development. 1964. 18 Int'l Org. 685-704.

Goodwin, G. L. The United Nations conference on trade and development: beginning of a new era? 1965. 19 Yb. World Aff. 1-25.

Haelen, A. van. La première année d'existence de l'UNCTAD. 1965. 30 Problèmes de l'Europe 27-41.

Hagras, Kamal M. United Nations conference on trade and development; a case study in U.N. diplomacy. New York, Praeger. 1965. 171p.

Hasselblatt, W. B. The world trade and development conference. Jan. 1964. Wirschaftsdienst (Hamburg) Monthly Rev. of Econ. Policy 9-14.

Hoffman, M. L. UNCTAD and the businessman. 1965. 7 Int'l Development Rev. 11-14.

Jeftić, Bora. Consultations of the 77 developing countries. April 20, 1966. 17 Rev. Int'l Aff. 18-20.

Johnson, G. Griffith. A perspective on the United Nations conference on trade and development. 1964. 50 Dep't State Bull. 410-15.

Kasdan, Alan Richard. Toward a reorganization of international trade—United Nations conference on trade and development. 1964. 19 Record 525-43.

Lacharrière, G. de. La conférence des Nations Unies sur le commerce et le développement; bilans et perspectives. 1964. 73 Rev. du Marché Commun 438-43.

Maes, A. La signification de la conférence des Nations Unies sur le commerce et le développement. Jan. 1965. 18 Chronique de Politique Etrangère 31-49.

Prebisch, Raúl.

    Portée de la conférence des Nations Unies sur le commerce et le développement—rapport adressé au secrétaire général des Nations Unies... July/Sept. 1964. 5 Tiers-Monde (Supp.) 1-16.

    Spirit of conciliation: the United Nations conference on trade and development: purposes and accomplishments. 1964. 1 U.N. Monthly Chronicle 71-77.

Proehl, P. O. The Geneva proposals to reform international trade: "a clear convergence of responsibilities." 1965. 33 Geo. Wash. L. Rev. 1031-66.

Shonfield, A. Trade as a tool of development; the issues at Geneva... 1964. 40 Int'l Aff. 219-31.

Silva, G. R. W. de. Problems of trade promotion of developing countries. 1965. 1 (1) Int'l Trade Forum 10-14.

Singer, H. W. The Geneva conference on trade and development. 1963/64. Ann. Rev. U. N. Aff. 47-79.

Stettner, Leonora. The U.N. conference on trade and development; Prebisch thesis and antithesis. Oct. 1964. 14 Cartel 140-53.

Subham, Malcolm. UNCTAD at work: emphasis on the discussions on possible measures to enable the developing nations to find overseas markets. April 1964. 44 Far East. Econ. Rev. 257-59.

Tough issues for new U.N. trade board: reviews work and surveys the unresolved issues that the new board will face. 1965. 115 Banker 230-35.

United Nations Conference on Trade and Development, Geneva, 1964.
Commercio e sviluppo. Padova, Cedam. 1965. 285pp.
Proceedings. New York, United Nations. 1964. 8v.
UNCTAD ... 1964. Doc. on Am. For. Relations 422-51.

United Nations. Office of Public Information. United Nations conference on trade and development, Geneva, 23 March-16 June 1964: I. A review of action taken by the conference, II. An appraisal of its impact on public opinion. New York. 1964. 54p.

United Nations. Trade and Development Board.
Comm. on Invisibles and Financing related to trade. Consideration of the adequacy of the rates of growth achieved by the developing countries: problems and issues: note by the secretary general of UNCTAD. Oct. 29, 1965. 12p.
Report of the United Nations conference on trade and development: annual report of the trade and development board to the General Assembly, Nov. 3, 1965. New York. 79p. (1965A/6023)

Weintraub, S. After the U.N. trade conference: lessons and portents. 1964. 43 For. Aff. 37-50.

Worsnop, R. L. World trade parleys. March 1964. Editorial Research Rep. (No. 10) 183-200.

COMMODITY AGREEMENTS

Action by governments to stabilise primary commodity prices. 1962. 85 Int'l Lab. Rev. 207-33.

Aubrey, H. G. International commodity markets as a factor in development planning. United Nations conference on the application of science and technology for the benefit of the less developed areas. 1962. 8 Sci., Technology & Development 55-67.

Baranyal, L. and Mills, J. C. International commodity agreements. Mexico, Centro de Estudios Monetarios Latinoamericanos. 1963. 190p.

Bauer, P. T. Issues in commodity stabilization in Africa (in Robinson, E. A. G., ed. Economic development for Africa south of the Sahara ... proceedings of a conference held by the International economic association. London, Macmillan, 1964, pp. 532-55)

Bauer, P. T. and Yamey, B. S. Organized commodity stabilization with voluntary participation. March 1964. 16 Oxford Econ. Pap. (n.s.) 105-13.

Benoit, Emile. Purchase guaranties as a means of reducing instability of commodity export proceeds of underdeveloped countries. 1959. 12 Kyklos (fasc. 3) 300-06.

Bilder, R. B. The international coffee agreement: a case history in negotiation. 1963. 28 Law & Contemp. Prob. 328-91.

Black, John D. and Tsou, S. S. International commodity arrangements. 1954. 58 Q. J. Econ. 521-52.

Blau, Gerda.
   International commodity arrangements and policies. 1963. 12 (9) Monthly Bull. of Agricultural Econ. & Statist. 1-9.
   International commodity arrangements and policies. Rome, Food and Agriculture Organization of the United Nations. 1964. 52p.
   International commodity arrangements (in Robinson, E. A. G., ed. Problems in economic development; proceedings in economic development; proceedings of a conference held by the International economic association. London, Macmillan, 1965, pp. 553-73)

Blau, Gerda and Music, D. A. Agricultural commodity trade and development prospects, problems and policies. Rome, Food and Agriculture Organization of the United Nations. 1964. 117p.

Blumenthal, W. M.
   Commodity trade and economic development. 1963. 48 Dep't State Bull. 844-48.
   International commodity problems. 1962. 46 Dep't State Bull. 997-1002.

Brandt, K. The failure of international commodity agreements. March 1965. 15 Freeman 12-21.

Brodie, Henry. Commodity agreements; a partial answer to the trade problems of developing countries. 1965. 53 Dep't State Bull. 111-17.

Caine, Sydney (Sir). Commodity agreements—a new look. Jan. 1963. 15 Lloyds Bank Rev. 14-29.

Chamber of Commerce of the United States. Comm. on Economic Policy. Commodity agreements—their role in the world economy: report. 1963. 46p.

Commodities and the underdeveloped countries. Aug. 1963. Westminster Bank Rev. 27-37.

109

Dantwala, M. L. Commodity terms of trade of primary producing countries (in Robinson, E. A. G., ed. Problems in economic development; proceedings of a conference held by the International economic association. London, Macmillan, 1965, pp. 498-509)

Dupriez, Léon H. Commodity and trade policy in Africa: the terms of trade of African producers (in Robinson, E. A. G., ed. Economic development for Africa south of the Sahara . . . proceedings of a conference held by the International economic association. London, Macmillan, 1964, pp. 503-31)

Ferrero, Romulo. Trade of the LDC's: no dead end for primary producers. Summer 1966. 1 Colum. J. World Bus. 51-62.

Gerhard, H. W. Commodity trade stabilization through international agreement. 1963. 28 Law & Contemp. Prob. 276-93.

Hanson, Simon G. The experience with the international coffee agreement. Winter 1965. 19 Inter-Am. Econ. Aff. 27-65.

Harbury, C. D. An experiment in commodity control—the international wheat agreement 1949-1953. Feb. 1954. 6 Oxford Econ. Pap. 82-97.

Haviland, W. E. International commodity agreements. Montreal, Canadian Trade Committee, Private Planning Association of Canada. 1963. 79p.

Hawkins, Robert G., Epstein, J. and Gonzales, J. Stabilization of export receipts and economic development—international commodity agreements and compensatory financing plans. N. Y. U., Graduate School of Business Administration, Institute of Finance Bull. No. 40 (Nov. 1966). 80p.

Hemmi, Kenzo. International commodity agreements: reality and the future. Dec. 1964. 2 Developing Econ. 358-72.

Heymann, H. The international tin scheme (in Robinson, E. A. G., ed. Problems in economic development; proceedings of a conference held by the International economic association. London, Macmillan, 1965, pp. 599-616)

Hooft-Welvaars, M. J. The organization of international markets for primary commodities (in United Nations conference on trade and development, Geneva, 1964. Proceedings vol. 3: Commodity trade. New York, 1964, pp. 458-521)

Hudson, S. C. and Gherson, Randolph. Competition in international trade with particular reference to agricultural commodities. Dec. 1958. 40 J. Farm Econ. 1717-28.

International commodity arrangements and policies: commodity export earnings and economic growth. 12 (12) Monthly Bull. Agricultural Econ. & Statist. 1-19.

International commodity arrangements—a story of slow but hopeful progress. Aug. 1966. Midland Bank Rev. (London) 11-13, 16-19.

International commodity price problems. Feb. 1962. Fed. Res. Chi. 8-16.

110

International organization of commodity trade. Feb. 1966. 15 Monthly Bull. Agricultural Econ. & Statist. 1-8.

Janton, Henri. L'organisation du marché des produits de base. Dec. 1965. Développement et Civilisations (No. 24) 19-24.

Kramme, R. D. International commodity agreements: purpose, policy and procedure. 1963. 31 Geo. Wash. L. Rev. 784-811.

Kruse-Rodenacker, A. Organization of world markets for agricultural commodities. Brussels. 1964. 52p.

Lacarte, J. A. The problem of primary commodity exports (in Robock, S. H. & Solomon, L. M., International development 1965. Dobbs Ferry, Oceana, 1966, pp. 167-73)

Liaqat, Ali. Principle of buffer stock and its mechanism and operation in the international tin agreement. 1966. 94 Weltwirtsch Archiv 141-87.

MacBean, Alasdair I. Export instability and economic development. Cambridge, Harvard Univ. Press. 1966. 367p.

Meade, J. E.
International commodity agreements. July 1964. Lloyds Bank Rev. 28-42.
International commodity agreements (in United Nations Conference on trade and development, Geneva, 1964. Proceedings vol. 3: commodity trade. New York, 1964, pp.451-57)

Mikesell, R. F.
Commodity agreements and aid to developing countries. 1963. 28 Law & Contemp. Prob. 294-312.
Commodity agreements and aid to developing countries (in Metzger, S. D. Law of international trade. Washington, 1966, pp. 1178-1201)

Nichols, C. W. Policy problems in international trade of agricultural products. 1964. 50 Dep't State Bull. 416-23.

Onitiri, H. M. A. The role of international organizations in developing African primary products (in Stewart, I. G. & Ord, H. W., eds. African primary products and international trade; papers delivered at an international seminar in the Univ. of Edinburgh, Sept. 1964. Edinburgh, University Press, 1965, pp.8-18)

Pincus, J. A.
Aid, trade and economic development: what policy for commodities? 1964. 42 For. Aff. 227-41.
Commodity agreements: bonanza or illusion? Jan/Feb. 1967. 2 Colum. J. World Bus. 41-50.

Principles of economic policy consistent and inconsistent: problems of international commodity stabilization. May 1963. 52 Am. Econ. Rev. 65-111.

Richter, J. H. Agricultural protection and trade: proposals for an international policy. New York, Praeger. 1964. 148p.

Rowe, J. W. F. Primary commodities in international trade. London, Cambridge, Univ. Press. 1965. 223p.

Schmidt, W. E. The case against commodity agreements. 1963. 28 Law & Contemp. Prob. 313-27.

Swerling, Boris C.
Current issues in commodity policy. Princeton, International Financial Section, Princeton University. 1962.
Financial alternatives to international commodity stabilization. Nov. 1964. Can. J. Econ. & Pol. Sci. 526-37.

Tarr, R. Bibliographie commentée. Le commerce international des produits de base et la stabilisation de leurs prix. 1961. 14 Problèmes de l'Europe 179-89.

United Nations. Economic Comm. for Africa. International action for commodity stabilization and the role of Africa. Nov. 5, 1960. 40p. (196E/CN.14/68)

Walker, H. The international law of commodity agreements. 1963. 28 Law & Contemp. Prob. 392-415.

COMPENSATORY FINANCING

Compensatory financing of export fluctuations. 1963. 3 (1) Central Bank Egypt Econ. Rev. 1-13.

Fund policies and procedures in relation to the compensatory financing of commodity fluctuations. 1960. 8 Int'l Monetary Fund Staff Pap. 1-76.

Grubel, Herbert G. The case against an international commodity reserve currency. March 1965. 17 Oxford Econ. Pap. 130-35.

Hart, Albert G. Monetary reform to further economic development. 1964. 79 Pol. Sci. Q. 360-77.

International Bank for Reconstruction and Development. Supplementary financial measure; a study requested by the United Nations conference on trade and development, 1964. Washington. 1965. 125p.

International Monetary Fund. Compensatory financing of export fluctuations: a report on compensatory financing of the fluctuations in exports of primary exporting countries. 1963. 27p.

Kindleberger, Charles P. Terms of trade for primary products (in Clawson, Marion, ed. Natural resources and international development. Baltimore, Johns Hopkins Press, 1964, pp. 339-65)

Kruse-Rodenacker, A. Organization of world markets for agricultural commodities; a joint action programme for developed and developing countries. Brussels, European Economic Community. 1964. 52p. (European Economic Community Studies, Agricultural series no. 15)

Lehti, Teuvo. Liquidity creation and the financing of commodity arrangements. March 1966. 15 Monthly Bull. Agricultural Econ. & Statist. 1-9.

Lovasy, Gertrud. Survey and appraisal of proposed schemes of compensatory financing. July 1965. 12 Int'l Monetary Fund Staff Pap. 189-223.

112

Morgan, D. J.
  International commodity problems and schemes for international compensatory financing. Dec. 1962. Banca Nazionale del Lavoro Q. Rev. 307-31.
  International compensatory financing applied to the Federation of Malaya and Singapore. 1962. 7 Malayan Econ. Rev. 64-76.
United Nations. Comm. on International Commodity Trade. Considerations of compensatory financial measures to offset fluctuations in the export income of primary producing countries; stabilization of export proceeds through a development insurance fund: study by the secretariat, Jan. 18, 1962. 191p. (1962 E/CN.13/43)
United Nations. Joint session of the U. N. commission on international commodity trade and FAO committee on commodity problems: International compensatory financing in relation to fluctuations in the price of primary commodities; application to individual commodities; a development insurance fund for single commodities; report by the U. N. secretariat, Feb. 6, 1962. 73p. (CE/CN.13/45)
United Nations. Department of Economic and Social Affairs. International compensation for fluctuations in commodity trade. New York. 1961. 96p.
United Nations. Dep't of Economic and Social Affairs. Export credits and developing financing. New York. 1967. 122p.
Wood, H. Commodity compensatory financing. 1963. 13 Cartel 109-15.

TARIFF PREFERENCES

Johnson, Harry G. Trade preferences and developing countries. April 1966. Lloyd Bank Rev. (no. 80) 1-18.
McNeill, Robert L. Tariff preferences for developing countries. 1966. 60 Am. Soc'y Int'l L. Proc. 93-102.
Mundell, R. A. Tariff preferences and the terms of trade. Jan. 1964. 32 Manchester Schl. of Econ. & Soc. Studies 1-13.
Ndegwa, Philip. Preferential trade arrangements among developing countries. Dec. 1965. 1 East African Econ. Rev. 1-22.
Patterson, Gardner. Would tariff preferences help economic developments? April 1965. 76 Lloyds Bank Rev. 18-30.
Les préférences; le rôle qu'elles pourraient jouer dans le cadre d'une politique d'aide à l'expansion commerciale des pays en voie de développement; un débat nouveau sur des thèmes anciens. Sept. 1965. 83 Rev. Marché Commun 371-75.
Rom, Michael. A suggestion for a preferential scheme in the developed countries for imports of manufacturers and semi-manufactures from developing countries. March 1966. 21 Aussenwirtschaft 43-53.

Sundara Rajan, K. S. Tariff preferences and developing countries. 1966. 60 Am. Soc'y Int'l L. Proc. 86-93.

Weintraub, Sidney. Trade preferences for less-developed countries. New York, Praeger. 1967. 225p.

GATT

Allen, James J. The European common market and the general agreement on tariff and trade: a study in compatibility. 1961. 26 Law & Contemp. Prob. 559-71.

Balensi, A. La technique des négociations au G.A.T.T. 1962. 47 Rev. du Marché Commun 193-98.

Catudal, H. M. The general agreement on tariffs and trade: an article-by-article analysis in layman's language. 1961. 44 Dep't State Bull. 1010-20; 45:35-42.

Charvet, L. Problèmes posés par la reprise des négociations tarifaires dans le cadre du GATT. Feb. 6, 1964. J. Officiel Avis et Rapports du Conseil Economique et Social 237-72.

Contracting Parties to the General Agreement on Tariffs and Trade.

The activities of GATT 1964/65. Nov. 1965. 42p.

Analysis of United States negotiations. Washington, Dep't of State. 1962. 3v.

Analysis of United States negotiations: 1960-61 tariff conference, Geneva. Washington, Gov't Print. Off. 1963. Vol. 4. 308p.

Basic instruments and selected documents: thirteenth supplement. 1965. 139p.

The developing countries and the Gatt: the new chapter on trade and development. Feb. 1965. 10p.

Final act authenticating the results of the 1960-61 tariff conference. Geneva. 1963. 88p.

Committee 2, GATT programme for expansion of international trade: trade in agricultural products; second and third reports. 1962. 49p .(Sales no.: GATT/1962.2)

GATT programme for expansion of international trade: trade of less-developed countries: special report. 1962. 60p. (Sales no.: GATT/1962-3)

International trade 1964. Geneva. 1965. 185p.

Report on the Geneva tariff negotiations 1960-62: with texts of the final act and the protocol to the general agreement on tariffs and trade emobdying results of the tariff conference. 1962. 12p.

The role of GATT in relation to trade and development. Geneva. 1964. 56p.

Trade of less-developed countries. Geneva. 1962. 60p.

Curzon, Gerald. Multilateral commercial diplomacy: an examination of the impact of the General agreement on tariffs and trade on national commercial policies and techniques. London, Michael Joseph. 1965. 367p.

Dam, K. W. Regional economic arrangements and the GATT: the legacy of a misconception. 1963. 30 U. Chi. L. Rev. 615-65.

Developing countries in GATT (in United Nations Conference on trade and development, Geneva, 1964. Proceedings. New York, 1964, Vol. 5, pp. 432-69)

Fisher, M. H. What chances of lower tariffs? GATT and the Kennedy round. 1963. 19 World Today 208-12.

Galbraith, V. The General agreement on tariffs and trade. 1962. 43 (251) Current History 23-38.

GATT and the developing countries. April 1965. 11 Nat'l & Grindlays Rev. 11-17.

Haves and have-nots. March 28, 1964. 150 New Republic 6-7.

Hoffman, M. L. Can the G.A.T.T. system survive? July 1964. Lloyds Bank Rev. 1-14.

An important declaration by GATT on the promotion of the trade of less-developed countries. 1962. 42 Inter-Parliamentary Bull. 26-30.

Issue facing GATT in the new trading world. 1962. 46 Dep't State Bull. 3-10.

Kunugi, T. State succession in the framework of GATT. 1965. 59 Am. J. Int'l L. 268-90.

Linder, S. B. The significance of GATT for under-developed and less-developed countries (in United Nations Conference on trade and development, Geneva, 1964. Proceedings, vol. 5, pp. 502-33)

Ramoin, R. The General agreement on tariffs and trade (G.A.T.T.). 1960. 87 J. du Droit International 731-60.

The role of GATT in relation to trade and development (in United Nations Conference on trade and development, Geneva, 1964. Proceedings, vol. 5, pp. 470-92)

Schwenger, Robert B. Synthesis of trade and agricultural policy in GATT. 1958. 40 J. Farm Econ. 238-48.

United States participation in the General agreement on tariffs and trade. 1961. 61 Colum. L. Rev. 505-69.

Vernon, Raymond A. America's foreign trade policy and GATT. Princeton, Princeton Univ. Press. 1954. 25p.

Weintraub, S. Border tax adjustments and the GATT. 1965. 17 Tax Executive 304-20.

White, Eric W. GATT as an international trade organization. Some structural problems of international trade. Geneva, Secretariat. 1961. 29p.

Willmann, J. La négociation Kennedy au G.A.T.T. 1964. Politique Etrangère 248-59.

Anselme-Rabinovitch, L. Les accords de coopération étape de l'intégration africaine. 1964. 3 Geneva-Africa 243-54.

L'association des états africains et malgache à la communauté économique européenne. Oct. 15, 1966. Documentation française, Notes et études documentaires no. 3327, 1-68.

Association of the Bar of the City of New York. Comm. on Foreign Law. Economic integration in Latin America. June 1962. 17 (6) Record Supp. 68p.

Balassa, Bela. Economic development and integration. Mexico, Centro de Estudios Monetarios Latinoamericanos. 1965. 157p.

Balogh, T. Africa and the common market. 1963. 1 J. Common Market Studies 79-112.

Borja Martínez, Francisco. Aspectos y consecuencias legales del tratado de Roma (Mercado Común Europeo), del tratado de Montevideo (Asociación Latino-Americana de Libre Comercio-ALALC), La Alianza para el progreso y otros programas de carácter regional. 1964. 10 Int'l B. A. Conf. 386-415.

Botero, Rodrígo. Una propuesta para acelerar la integración económica en América Latina. 1966. 39 Banco de la República, Revista (Bogotá) 1390-94.

Bruyas, J. La convention de Yaoundé, charte de l'association condue entre la C.E.E. et dix-huit états africains et malgache, 20 juillet 1963. 1965. Annales Africaines 129-72.

Cardosi, G. Movimenti di integrazione economica in Africa. 1964. Riv. Internazionale di Scienze Sociali 473-83.

Dell, Sidney. Experiencias de la integración económica en América Latina. Mexico, Cemba. 1966. 374p.

Dell, Sidney. Trade blocs and common markets. New York, Knopf. 1963. 384p.

Diab, M. The Arab common market. 1966. 4 J. Common Market Studies 238-50.

Farag, A. Economic integration in Latin America. Nov. 1963. 16 Economia Internazionale 714-24.

Fernández-Shaw, F. Estado actual de la integración económica centroamericana. Nov/Dec. 1964. Rev. de Política Internacional 76-106.

Galan Sarmiento, L. C. and Gutiérrez, R. Echeverry. Integración económica latinoamericana. June 1966. Universitas 90-113.

García Reynoso, Plácido. Integración económica latino-americana, primera etapa 1960-1964. Mexico, D. F. Publicaciones Especializadas. 1965. 282p.

Gardiner, R. K. Integrated economic development in Africa—the role of the Economic commission. June 1965. 7 Int'l Development Rev. 7-10.

Garnick, D. H. Regional integration and economic development in the middle east. 1961. 12 Middle East. Aff. 294-300.

Hafez, H. The proposed Arab common market. Dec. 1964. 9 Scribe 37-39.

Harrod, Roy. Economic development and Asian regional cooperation 1962. 2 Pakistan Development Rev. 1-22.

Harrod, Roy and Hague, Douglas C., eds. International trade theory in a developing world. London, Macmillan. 1963. 571p.

Hass, Ernst B. and Schmitter, Philippe C. The politics of economics in Latin American regionalism: the Latin American free trade association after four years of operation. Denver, Univ. of Denver Press. 1965. 78p.

Hazlewood, A. The East African common market—importance and effects Feb. 1966. 28 Bull. Oxford U. Inst. of Econ. & Statist. 1-18.

Herrera, Felipe.
América latina integrada. Losada, S.A., Buenos Aires. 1964. 240p.
Aspectos políticos e económicos da integracao da América Latina. March 1965. 8 Rev. Brasileira de Política Internacional 22-45.

Herrera, Felipe, Mayobre, Antonio, Prebisch Raúl and Sanz de Santamaría, Carlos. Proposals for the creation of the Latin American common market. Sept. 1966. 5 J. Common Market Studies 83-110.

Hirschman, Albert O., ed. Latin American issues: essays and comments. New York, Twentieth Century Fund. 1961. 201p.

Huelin, David. Economic integration of Latin-America—progress and problems. 1964. 40 Int'l Aff. 430-39.

L'intégration économique de l'Amerique latine. Sept/Oct. 1966. Banque Française et Italienne pour l'Amerique du Sud 3-52.

Islam, Nurul. Regional co-operation for development: Pakistan, Iran and Turkey. 1967. 5 J. Common Market Studies 283-301.

Khan, M. A. A plea for Asian common market. March 1962. 10 Pakistan Rev. 23.

La integración latinoamericana: situación y perspectivas. Buenos Aires, Instituto para la Integración de América Latina. 1965. 217p.

Lagos, G. Aspectos políticos, legales e institucionales de la integración económica de América Latina. June 1966. Boletín de la Integración 2-10.

Leduc, M. Note sur les marchés communs africains. 1962. 2 Annales Africaines 370-82.

Lim, M. Regional and international cooperation for facilitating economic development, April/May 1966. 16 Indus. Philippines 25-34.

Manzanares, H. La convención de asociación de los estados africanos y malgache a la C.E.E. May/June 1965. Rev. Política Internacional 91-105.

117

Mills, Joseph C. La política de desarrollo y los convenios regionales decomercio: el caso de América Latina. July/Sept. 1963. 30 El Trimestre Económico 383-96.

Mundell, R. A. Tariff preferences and the terms of trade. Jan. 1964. 32 Manchester School of Econ. & Social Studies 1-13.

Papisca, A. Le organizzazioni latino-americane di cooperazione economica. 1966. 20 (1) Diritto Internazionale, Parte 1a 42-96.

Perloff, Harvey S. and Almeida, Romulo. Regional economic integration in the development of Latin America. Nov. 1963. 1 (2) Economía Latinoamericana 150-79.

Prebisch, Raúl. Toward a dynamic development policy for Latin America. New York, United Nations. 1963. 103p. (E/CN.12/680/Rev.)

Razafimbahny, J. A. L'association des pays africains et malgache au marché commun européen. 1963. Rev. Juridique et Politique d'Outre-Mer 177-201.

Rifaat, M. A. Afro-Asian organisation for economic co-operation (AFRASEC). 1965. 15 (1) Civilisations 73-78.

Segal, Aaron. The integration of developing countries: some thoughts on East Africa and Central America. 1967. 5 J. Common Market Studies 252-82.

Singh, Lalita Prasad. The politics of economic cooperation in Asia: a study of Asian international organizations. Columbia, Univ. of Missouri Press. 1966. 271p.

Urquidi, Víctor L. Free trade and economic integration in Latin America. Berkeley, Univ. of California Press. 1962. 190p.

Urquidi, Víctor L. The challenge of development in Latin America. New York, Praeger. 1960. 209p.

Ustunel, B. Western regionalism and developing countries. 1963. Turkish Yb. Int'l Relations 63-80.

Vieira, M. A. L'association latino-américaine de libre commerce (A.L.A.L.C.), ses principaux aspects juridique. 1966. 93 J. du Droit Int'l 617-21.

Wionczek, Miguel S., ed. La integración de América Latina: experiencias y perspectivas. Mexico, Fondo de Cultura Económica, Mexico. 1964. 381p.

Wood, R. N. The East African common market; a reassessment. 1966. Oxford U. Inst. of Econ. & Statist. Bull. 273-79.